THE LIBRARY OF HOLOCAUST TESTIMONIES

The Jews of Poznań

The Library of Holocaust Testimonies

My Lost World by Sara Rosen
From Dachau to Dunkirk by Fred Pelican
Breathe Deeply, My Son by Henry Wermuth
My Private War by Jacob Gerstenfeld-Maltiel
A Cat Called Adolf by Trude Levi
An End to Childhood by Miriam Akavia
A Child Alone by Martha Blend
The Children Accuse by Maria Hochberg-Marianska and Noe Gruss
I Light a Candle by Gena Turgel
My Heart in a Suitcase by Anne L. Fox
Memoirs from Occupied Warsaw, 1942–1945
by Helena Szereszewska
Have You Seen My Little Sister?
by Janina Fischler-Martinho
Surviving the Nazis, Exile and Siberia by Edith Sekules
Out of the Ghetto by Jack Klajman with Ed Klajman
From Thessaloniki to Auschwitz and Back
by Erika Myriam Kounio Amariglio
Translated by Theresa Sundt
I Was No. 20832 at Auschwitz by Eva Tichauer
Translated by Colette Lévy and Nicki Rensten
My Child is Back! by Ursula Pawel
Wartime Experiences in Lithuania by Rivka Lozansky Bogomolnaya
Translated by Miriam Beckerman
Who Are You, Mr Grymek? by Natan Gross
Translated by William Brand
A Life Sentence of Memories by Issy Hahn, Foreword by Theo Richmond
An Englishman in Auschwitz by Leon Greenman
For Love of Life by Leah Iglinsky-Goodman
No Place to Run: The Story of David Gilbert by Tim Shortridge and
Michael D. Frounfelter
A Little House on Mount Carmel by Alexandre Blumstein
From Germany to England Via the Kindertransports by Peter Prager
By a Twist of History: The Three Lives of a Polish Jew by Mietek Sieradzki
The Jews of Poznań by Zbigniew Pakula
Lessons in Fear by Henryk Vogler
To Forgive … But Not Forget by Maja Abramowitch

The Jews of Poznań

ZBIGNIEW PAKULA

translated by William Brand

VALLENTINE MITCHELL
LONDON • PORTLAND, OR

First published in 2003 in Great Britain by
VALLENTINE MITCHELL
Crown House, 47 Chase Side, Southgate
London N14 5BP

and in the United States of America by
VALLENTINE MITCHELL
c/o ISBS, 5824 N. E. Hassalo Street
Portland, Oregon 97213-3644

Website: www.vmbooks.com

Copyright © 2003 Zbigniew Pakula

British Library Cataloguing in Publication Data
Pakula, Zbigniew
     The Jews of Poznan. – (The library of Holocaust testimonies)
     1. Holocaust, Jewish (1939–1945) – Poland – Poznan 2. Jews –
     Poland – Poznan – History – 20th century 3. Poznan (Poland)
     – History – 20th century
     I. Title
     940.5'318'094384

     ISBN 0-85303-430-3 (paper)
     ISSN 1363-3759

Library of Congress Cataloging-in-Publication Data
Pakula, Zbigniew, 1952–
     The Jews of Poznan / Zbigniew Pakula; translated by William Brand.
         p. cm. – (Library of Holocaust testimonies, ISSN 1363-3759)
     ISBN 0-85303-430-0 (pbk.)
         1. Jews–Poland–Poznań–History. 2. Holocaust, Jewish (1939–1945)–Poland–
     Poznań. 3. Holocaust survivors–Biography. 4. Poznań (Poland)–Ethnic relations.
     I. Title. II. Series

DS135.P62 P6357 2002
940.53'18'0943849–dc21

                                                                    2002026511

Typeset in 11/12.25pt Palatino by Frank Cass Publishers Ltd, London
Printed and bound in Great Britain by
MPG Books Ltd, Victoria Square, Bodmin, Cornwall

Contents

The Library of Holocaust Testimonies

It is greatly to the credit of Frank Cass that this series of survivors' testimonies is being published in Britain. The need for such a series has been long apparent, where many survivors made their homes.

Since the end of the war in 1945 the terrible events of the Nazi destruction of European Jewry have cast a pall over our time. Six million Jews were murdered within a short period; the few survivors have had to carry in their memories whatever remains of the knowledge of Jewish life in more than a dozen countries, in several thousand towns, in tens of thousands of villages, and in innumerable families. The precious gift of recollection has been the sole memorial for millions of people whose lives were suddenly and brutally cut off.

For many years, individual survivors have published their testimonies. But many more have been reluctant to do so, often because they could not believe that they would find a publisher for their efforts.

In my own work over the past two decades I have been approached by many survivors who had set down their memories in writing, but who did not know how to have them published. I also realized, as I read many dozens of such accounts, how important each account was, in its own way, in recounting aspects of the story that had not been told before, and adding to our understanding of the wide range of human suffering, struggle and aspiration.

With so many people and so many places involved, including many hundreds of camps, it was inevitable that the historians and students of the Holocaust should find it difficult at times to grasp the scale and range of events. The publication of memoirs is therefore an indispensable part of the extension of knowledge, and of public awareness of the crimes that had been committed against a whole people.

Sir Martin Gilbert
Merton College, Oxford

Introduction

Rest here

After the Jews had been expelled from Germany, a popular legend has it that the Lord showed them a hospitable land on the Rivers Warta and Vistula, saying to them: *'Po-lin'* (in Hebrew, this means 'rest here'). For historians, however, it is no easy task to identify the beginnings of Jewish settlement in Wielkopolska region. The date most commonly given is around the year 1200, and most researchers link this settlement to the persecution of the Jews in Western Europe. There is another interesting theory about Jewish settlement, associated with 'settlement fever' – the term applied to the thirteenth-century expansion of the German population, when they founded cities and agricultural colonies in the Polish lands.

The Kalisz Statute

The oldest and most certain evidences of Jewish presence are coins minted on the orders of Mieszko III the Elder. There is also an extant funerary inscription in Wrocław, dated 1203, for one David, son of Sar Shalom. The oldest royal privilege for the founding of a Jewish cemetery in Wielkopolska region dates from 1287. It is agreed that Jewish people settled first in Silesia, the Wielkopolska region and the Kujawy region. Undoubtedly the most significant event for Jewish settlement in the Wielkopolska region was the decision of the Prince of Kalisz, Bolesław the Pious, to grant immunity privileges to the Jews in 1264. He declared them to be free people, guaranteed the protection of their prayer houses and cemeteries, and granted them judicial autonomy. In 1334 Kazimierz the Great extended Bolesław's privileges over all of Poland. He modelled the Kalisz Statute on the privileges granted to the Jews of Austria by Frederick II the Warlike, and to the Jews of Bohemia by Premyslav Otokar II. The Statute originally contained six articles, along with an injunction to Christians to come to the aid of the Jews in case of nocturnal assault. The Statute confirmed Innocent IV's 1253 Bull: 'that in the future no one accuse any Jew residing in our state of consuming human blood since, according to the dictates of the Law, all Jews should absolutely refrain from consuming any sort of blood'.

The Jewish district

The 1253 municipal privileges of Poznań make no mention of the Jews. Perhaps they were regarded as the prince's people, and therefore not subject to municipal law. Ignacy Schiper, the most eminent historian of the Polish Jews, assumes that the Jewish community of Poznań is older than that of Kalisz, without offering any proof in support of his thesis. If Jews lived in Poznań in the thirteenth century, then under the provisions of the Synod of Wrocław they would have been assigned a separate district, a quarter, in which to live. Only from the fifteenth century do we have more information about the existence of such a district. The quarter was then formed by Sukiennicza Street (renamed Ulica Żydowska – Jewish Street – in the late fifteenth century), Szewska Street and part of Wroniecka Street. This was not a walled ghetto. Nor was the ban on renting nearby Christian-owned houses to Jews enforced. Significantly, it is precisely in this part of the city that Jewish life in Poznań was concentrated throughout the centuries, until the outbreak of the Second World War.

In the fifteenth century there were still few Jewish houses. Historical sources indicate that Eustachy Kot bought a house from Moses the Jew in 1443, that Jan Nuczka sold a house to Salomon in 1460 and that Jonasz the Jew sold his house to Jakub, a Jew from Koźmin, nine years later. A contract for the digging of a well in the Jewish district, dated 1464, has also survived. The stone mason Jakub, who was awarded the contract, received 40 grzywien for his work.

2

Courts, schools and characters

The sources first mention Jewish courts in the year 1400. Sessions were held that year in the house of Abraham the Jew, and the following year in the house of Muszka the Jew. The Poznań Talmudic school, Lamdei Pozna, was famous in the late fifteenth century. According to the historian Perles, its most renowned scholars and teachers included Rabbi Jorna Turek, Moses of Halle, Pinkas of Vienna, Rabbi Juda of Obornik and Isaac Mintz (an exile from Germany).

The moneylenders of Poznań were, like the scholars, well-known figures. The moneylender Aaron was active in the city from 1386 to 1400. His sons Abraham, Isaac and Israel, along with his son-in-law Daniel, worked in his office. Another prominent figure, especially popular among the nobility, was the moneylender Jordan. He was in business from 1387 to 1416, assisted by his wife and his son Abraham. Other money-lenders were Muszko Bogacz (with his sons Abraham and Lazar), Manlin (with his daughter Jochna) and the Benaszes (husband and wife).

Among the notable characters of fifteenth-century Poznań, mention must also be made of the robber Słoma and the troublemaker Jonah of Sambor. The latter beat up so many Jews and Christians that, when he confessed his guilt in 1457, he was banished from the city under pain of death at the urging of the Jewish community. A year later, however, Jonah returned. This time, his fellow Jews saved him from death by requesting his pardon. He was banished to a distance of 40,000 paces from the city.

Another Jewish native of Poznań was a man who met Vasco da Gama in India, converted to Christianity and, under the name Gaspar da Gama, accompanied the great explorer on his voyage back to Portugal.

The Old Synagogue and the New Synagogue

According to tradition, the first synagogue in Poznań was founded in 1367, somewhere near the present-day intersection of Szewska and Dominikańska Streets. The earliest original documents, however, date from 1449, and it is not known if they deal with the same synagogue mentioned in the earlier reports. The first reference to a Jewish cemetery, probably located in the vicinity of the Dominican cloisters, is dated 1438.

The scholars associated with the Lamdei Pozna school took the initiative in founding the next synagogue. This so-called 'New Prayer House' stood between Żydowska, Wroniecka and Mokra Streets. The complex of community synagogue buildings that arose on that site was not demolished until 1908. The building was erected of brick and stones, and resembled a single-nave medieval church with a sharply pitched roof. The original synagogue had only a room for men. Porches and a gallery for women were added later.

The beginnings of the construction of the 'New Prayer House', in the late sixteenth century, coincided with a rise in the number of Jewish immigrants to Poznań and other Polish cities. At the same time, the appearance of the Jewish district was changing. Almost the whole quarter burned down in 1590. King Zygmunt III Vasa ordered that it be rebuilt in brick. The 'New Synagogue' was finished in 1618. On its north side, it adjoined two women's prayer houses belonging to the Old Synagogue. A prayer house known as Nehemiah's Synagogue (in fact an extension of the front of the house at 21 Żydowska Street) closed off the courtyard between the Old and New Synagogues.

In the mid nineteenth century both synagogues underwent a general renovation. Gas illumination was installed at this time. By 1880, however, the buildings had reached the point of collapse and the construction police wanted to close them. At that point, the community approved further renovation and appropriated 70,000 marks to carry it out.

The Corpus Christi legend

The Poznań legend of the profanation of the host dates from 1399. It stems from accusations that began to gain currency in the thirteenth century. A miracle that occurred in Paris in 1290 was the turning-point. According to the Parisian accusation, the moneylender Jonathan promised a Christian woman in his debt that he would return the garments she had pawned – on condition that she supply him with a eucharistic host. Desirous of seeing the blood hidden within the wafer, Jonathan pricked it. The host bled. Jonathan then tore the host into pieces and boiled it in olive oil. Despite such treatment, the host reconstituted itself and then divided into three parts. This story spawned at least 50 similar charges. The Poznań legend fits the pattern.

There are several versions of what happened in Poznań, the most popular of which is based on the following story. A certain woman retained the host in her mouth after taking communion, and then sold it to the Jews. They took the host to a cellar (allegedly the cellar of the Świdwy house on Żydowska Street), where they 'crucified' it by piercing it with knives until 'the blood of Christ spurted out'. Finally, after unsuccessful attempts to burn it or sink it in the river, they cast it into a meadow. The host rose into the air, the cattle knelt before it and a shepherd found it. The Church of Corpus Christi, endowed by King Władysław Jagiełło, was built at that site and still stands.

The spreading of legends about the profanation of the host caused growing anxiety in the Jewish communities. After several Jews were executed on similar charges in the so-called 'Sochaczew Trial', King Zygmunt August guaranteed the security of all the Jews residing in Poland. The Poznań Jewish community received a separate privilege of royal protection in 1556. In January of the following year, King Zygmunt August forbade the municipal court in Poznań to imprison Jews, on pain of a fine of 100 grzywien. When the old accusations reared their head in the city again, the king issued a document assuring the Jews that charges of ritual murder and profanation of the host could be judged only by royal officials.

Later synagogues

The first Reformed synagogue (known as the Temple of the Association of the Community of Brethren) was built in 1856–57. It was situated on the corner of Dominikańska and

Szewska Streets, across from the Dominican church. The property adjacent to the Temple was purchased at the same time. A house for the rabbi and cantor, and a weekday synagogue, were built there. The Jewish intelligentsia and bourgeoisie of nineteenth-century Poznań made up most of the congregation of the new Community of Brethren Temple.

The Orthodox segment of the Jewish community continued to be linked to the synagogue at 15–18 Żydowska Street. In its dilapidated condition, the old synagogue cried out to be replaced. A commission convened by I. Friedlaender put forth such a proposal in 1902. They invited bids for a design, and subsequently chose the project submitted by the Berlin firm of Cremer & Wolffenstein. The cornerstone was laid on 6 March 1906. Construction went on for 18 months. The dedication of the new synagogue, which could hold a thousand people, took place on 5 September 1907. The building was laid out on the plan of a symmetrical cross, with an enormous dome covered in copper sheeting. The design combined Romanesque and Moorish elements. This was the only synagogue in Poznań to survive the Second World War. The Germans converted it into a swimming pool during the Occupation, and it continues to fill that role to the present day. Only in 1989 was a plaque, funded by an American businessman, attached to its walls to recall the original function of the building. The plaque disappeared from the building in 1997.

The rabbis of Poznań

As early as the fifteenth century, Poznań, Cracow, Lwów and Lublin formed the so-called 'Tetrapolis'. In 1581 this was transformed into the Sejm (or parliament) of the Four Lands (Vaad Arba Aracot). Throughout 1764 this collegial assembly functioned as the supreme authority for all the Jewish communities in Poland. The Rabbi of Poznań sat in this body as the Rabbi of the Wielkopolska region, which indicates the high esteem attached to his position. However, the community statutes forbade Poznań natives from serving as rabbi of the city. Popular figures from elsewhere, even from outside Poland, were thus invited to fill the position.

The first rabbi whose name we know was Pechno, who headed the community from 1389 to 1393. Another popular rabbi was Moses Minz (Menz?), the head of the Lamdei Pozna Talmud school from 1474–1508. Eliezer Aszkenazi ben EliaRofe was appointed rabbi in 1580. He had studied in Salonika and had become a rabbi in Egypt. After 22 years, he moved to Venice, and thence to Prague. He was rabbi of Poznań for only a year. Another famous rabbi was Juda Loew ben Becaleel, also known as the High Rabbi Loew, or MaHaRal of Prague. He was born in Poznań, and his uncle Jakub ben Chaim of Worms served as head rabbi of all the communities in the German empire. Three of his descendants occupied the chair of the Poznań rabbis. He himself was a legendary figure. As a cabalist and rabbi of Prague, he is said to be the one who brought the Golem to life.

Loew's friend Mordechai ben Abraham Jaffe also held the chair of rabbi of Poznań. His descendants were still in Poznań in the early twentieth century, and it is to the photographer Samuel Jaffe that we owe the pictures of the old synagogue on Żydowska Street, which was pulled down in 1908.

Numerous misfortunes befell the Poznań community in the mid seventeenth century. The Jews were accused of collaborating with the enemy during the Swedish wars, and became the victims of pogroms at the hands of the army and the residents of the city. Nevertheless, the Jews made up a significant part of the population – 32.3 per cent in the 1670s. The proportion of Jewish residents was higher only in Wronki (52.7 per cent) and Kalisz (36.7 per cent). One of the most colourful figures of the period was Rabbi Naftali ben Isaac Ka-Kohen of Ostrów, who achieved fame as a cabalist.

The most famous of the Poznań rabbis was Akiba Eiger, who was entrusted with the spiritual leadership of the community in 1815. Eiger was born in Austria and displayed a talent for the Talmud at an early age. Itzhik Margolioth of Leszno was so taken by Eiger's wisdom that he gave him the hand of his daughter in marriage, and then decided to finance all of his son-in-law's material needs, so that Eiger could devote himself fully to his studies. Akiba Eiger became renowned as an opponent of Jewish reform, and successfully opposed the abolition of the *cheder* schools in 1833. He died on

12 October 1837, at the age of seventy-six. He is depicted in a painting, *The Poznań Square in 1838*, by Julius Knorr. Akiba's son, Salomon Eiger, succeeded his father after the latter's death.

In the mid nineteenth century the rabbinical chair of Poznań was held by Salomon Plessner, a defender of Orthodox Judaism who carried on Akiba Eiger's work. Yet liberal and reform tendencies were becoming increasingly widespread at this time, and the opponents of Orthodoxy founded a new body, the Community of Brethren, which went on to build its own temple. In 1862 the Community of Brethren appointed a rabbi of its own, Joseph Perles. Plessner's followers, in turn, founded the Unity Community.

When Perles left to take up the post of rabbi of Munich, he was succeeded by Philipp Bloch. Bloch remained in office until 1921 when, at the age of eighty, he moved to Berlin along with other Jewish people who did not feel themselves to be a part of the newly independent Polish state. The Unity rabbi until 1913 was Wolf Feilchenfeld. Jakob Freimann succeeded him. In 1928 Freimann went off to Berlin to be the rabbi there. Afterwards, the chair of the rabbi of Poznań remained vacant for several years. Beginning in 1929, the community was led by assistant rabbi Dawid Szyje Sender (who had previously lived in Konin). A competition for the post of rabbi was not held until 1935: Sender, who stood unopposed, won. We know nothing about his fate during the war. Like most of the Jews of Poznań who were deported from the city in December 1939, he probably died.

Assimilation

Until the end of the eighteenth century the Jews of Poznań and the Wielkopolska region lived at a distance from the Christians. This isolation resulted from their legal status, as well as from their religious and cultural distinctness. Under the influence of an Enlightenment movement called Haskala this isolation began to break down. Proponents of Haskala became more frequent in Poznań, and the Prussian authorities began to pay attention to their aims. An emancipation edict granting numerous civil rights to the Jews of the Prussian provinces was issued in 1812. Initially, their coreligionists in Wielkopolska region looked forward to benefiting from a similar measure. However, they had to wait until 1833 for the promulgation of the 'Provisional Decree in Regard to Jewry'. This edict divided the Jews into two categories: naturalized and tolerated. The former were granted civil rights, while the latter had to earn those rights. The Prussian authorities adopted this strategy in order to accelerate the assimilation of the Jews into the urban German middle class.

The decree permitted naturalized Jews to vote and stand as candidates in local council and mayoral elections. At first, however, nothing was done to encourage such participation. Only in 1846, when the Germans became concerned about the need for a counterweight to the Poles, did the first two Jewish council members cross the threshold of Poznań City Hall. From then on, they were able to tip the political balance between the Poles and the Germans. Eventually, they began moving closer towards the Germans in cultural terms, maintaining a loyalty to the Prussian state that had granted their rights. The Poles paid little attention at first. As Polish aspirations to independence grew, however, they were accompanied by mistrust of the Jews. In this way, the Jews found themselves at the very centre of the nineteenth-century Polish–German conflict.

1848: the 'Springtime of the Peoples'

Poznań and the Wielkopolska region were caught up in the ferment of 1848. However, the Jews had an ambivalent attitude towards the 'Springtime of the Peoples'. Historians often describe their sentiments as pro-German, but the truth is actually more complex. When the Polish National Committee issued a proclamation guaranteeing respect for Jewish rights on 22 March 1848, the Jewish representatives, Eduard Katz and Joseph Samter, immediately declared their support for the Polish cause. Jews began joining local National Guard units. However, the National Committee refused to accept Jews from Poznań as members. Within five days the Germans founded their own National Committee, and the Jews once again found themselves in the middle of the ethnic strife. The majority made no effort to conceal their pro-German leanings. At the same time, more than a dozen Jews died in numerous anti-Jewish riots in and around Poznań. Crowds attacked shops, homes and synagogues. In several localities (such as Krotoszyn and Leszno), the Jews in turn prevented the Poles from taking control of towns.

It is worth remembering that many Jewish physicians supported the Polish side in 1848. One of the best known was Marcus Mosse of Grodzisko Wielkopolski, who joined the Polish Committee in Buk. When Prussian hussars attempted to storm Grodzisk from the direction of the village of Doktorowo on 28 April 1848, it was Mosse who commanded the defence. Other physicians acted in a similar way. Township surgeon Brodsak of Września attended to the casualties at Miłosław. Ehrlich Loebel was a member of the Polish Committee in Jarocin, and Eliasz Wachtel cared for wounded partisans at the Battle of Książ.

Famous scholars and scientists

Many people born in Poznań in the nineteenth century went on to achieve fame, usually at German universities, as scholars and scientists. They included Jerzy Adler (1863–1908), a professor at the University of Cologne. Adler was a proponent of the school of ethical economics, and a critic of Marx's 'scientific socialism'. Behrend Pick, born in Poznań in 1861, became professor of archaeology at the University of Zurich, and was regarded as a pre-eminent numismatist. Meyer Hamburger (1838–1903), professor of mathematics at the Charlottenburg Technical Hochschule, formed an original theory of differential equations. Hermann Caro of Poznań (1834–1910) played a key role in the development of the German dyestuffs industry, inventing a wide range of synthetic dyes. Herman Munk (1839–1912), professor at the School of Veterinary Medicine in Berlin, was a member of the German Academy and won fame for his research into the functioning of the brain.

The first Jewish *docent* at the University of Berlin was Robert Rema (1815–65). He made important discoveries in regard to the neural fibres and pioneered the use of electrical current to treat neurological disorders. His Poznań colleague at the same university, Herman Senator (1834–1911), won fame for his study of the consequences of diseases in marriage.

Many famous Jewish figures came from the Wielkopolska region near Poznań. Izydor Kalisz (Isidor Kalish), born in Krotoszyn in 1817, became the rabbi of Cleveland, wrote an introduction to the Talmud, and translated the mystical Sefer Yetzira into English. Adolf Warschauer, born in Kępno in 1855, went on to become director of the Prussian State Archive in Danzig (Gdańsk). Henryk (Heinrich) Graetz (1817–91) was born in Książ. The greatest historian of the Jewish people, he was despised by Prussian historians for awakening the Jewish spirit. Natives of Rawicz include Markus Brann (1849–1920), author of a history of the Jews of Silesia, and Alfred Loewy, author of an algebra textbook and of studies of actuarial calculations. Another native of the Wielkopolska region was the Nobel Prize laureate Albert Michelson (1852–1933), who was born in Strzelno and became a professor of physics at the University of Chicago. Michelson measured the wavelength of light and proved that the 'ether' is unmoving relative to the earth. Ismar Boas, born near Poznań, opened the first clinic in the world specializing in diseases of the stomach and intestines, and was known as the most brilliant pathologist of his day.

Problems of identity

When the Second Polish Republic was established in 1918, many Jewish people felt a greater affinity for German culture, and wanted Poznań to remain within the borders of Germany. Many of them therefore headed for Germany when Polish freedom-fighters liberated the city. The newspaper *Orędownik* stated that 1,047 of the 5,144 Polish Jews who opted for Germany came from Poznań. They were not, however, as quick to leave Poznań as were non-Jewish Germans. Leading community figures such as Dr Max Kollenscher called on the Jews to remain in Poznań. Nevertheless, Kollenscher himself soon left for Germany. Emigration did not have a significant effect on the Jewish population in Poznań, since other Jews were constantly arriving from the former Austrian and Russian zones in hopes of finding better living conditions. In 1926, for instance, 144 Jews moved out of Poznań while 325 moved in. Zbigniew Dworecki states that not more than 15 per cent of the Jews living in Poznań in early 1931 had lived there before Polish independence.

According to the official statistics, 5,611 residents of Poznań (3.6 per cent of the total population) in 1910 were Jewish, 2,131 (1.2 per cent) in 1921, 1,410 (0.7 per cent) in 1929, and 1,954 (0.79 per cent) in 1931. The membership rolls of the Jewish Religious Community indicate that far higher numbers of people regarded themselves as Jewish in the religious sense. There were 1,650 of them in 1930, 2,300 in 1933, 2,700 in 1937, 2,800 in 1938, and approximately 3,000 in the year when the war broke out. At any given time there must have been several hundred additional people who had not registered.

The district

Between the First and Second World Wars, Jews most commonly lived in the so-called 'lower downtown', which included the Old Town Square and Żydowska, Wrocławska, Dominikańska, Szewska, Wroniecka, Kramarska, Wielka, Kozia, Wodna, Małe Garbary, and Wielkie Garbary Streets. A good number also lived in 'upper downtrown', on Wielkopolski Square, Marcinkowski Avenue, and Św. Martin, 27 Grudnia, and Ratajczaka Streets. Jewish families could also be found in the Łazarz and Jeżycach districts.

The Jewish Religious Community

Originally named the Israelite Religious Community, the organization went under the name Jewish Religious Community after 1933. It was one of 11 such bodies that were

12

active in the province of Poznań before the war, and included the city and the surrounding township. Under the law of 6 March 1928, the Community was required to support the office of the rabbi, the synagogue, the cemetery and other buildings connected with religious practice. It had corporate legal status and was free to buy and sell property. The members were required to pay fees. The poor were entitled to receive material aid.

The chairman of the Community was a Zionist attorney named Marcin Cohn. The majority of the members came from families that had lived in Poznań since before Polish independence.

The Community had about 20 employees including the rabbi, the community secretary, cantors, a ritual slaughterer, the synagogue chancellor, a teacher for the religious school, and workers at the cemetery and baths. Apart from fees levied on its members, the Community had income from the synagogue (for weddings, for instance), the cemetery (for the right to erect gravestones), from the baths and from the rental of apartments in buildings owned by the Community.

Among the property that the Community owned, the two synagogues on Stawna Street and at 8 Dominikańska and 4–5 Szewska Streets were assessed in 1938 at a value of 630,000 złoty. There were also several apartment buildings and an administrative building that included a library, religious school, and the rabbi's apartment. Other property included the cemetery on Focha Street (now Głogowska Street), the Jewish Home for Orphan Girls at 3 Noskowski Street, and the A. and H. Rohr Foundation Jewish Hospital at 4–5 Wały Wazów Street (now Wieniawski Street).

Other Jewish institutions with important functions included the Salomon ben Latz Foundation Shelter for the Aged and Infirm at 15–18 Żydowska Street, and the Baron Kottwitz Foundation Jewish Orphanage at 5 Stawna Street. The numerous charitable organizations included the Israelite Nursing Care and Funeral Association, the Poznań Jewish Women's Aid Union and Achi Eser: the Society for Aid to Poor Jews.

Merchants and craftsmen

Most of the Jews of prewar Poznań belonged to the petty bourgeoisie. After 1919 it was primarily wealthy burghers, intellectuals and officials who emigrated to Germany. The economic situation for the Jewish petty bourgeoisie in Poznań was better than in other regions of Poland. This made people eager to settle there. In 1935 approximately 55 per cent of the Jews were merchants. Shop assistants and door-to-door salesmen probably brought the proportion of those engaged in commerce to something near 70 per cent. The list of electors of the new rabbi in 1935 contained 54 per cent merchants, 13 per cent craftsmen, 10 per cent intellectuals and bureaucrats, and 5.5 per cent workers. In 1933 Jews owned approximately 200 shops, of which the largest number (60 shops) sold men's and women's clothing. There were also shops that were owned by Jews but officially run by Poles. There were two Jewish-owned banks: the Shareholders' Bank on Szewska Street and the Commercial Bank on December 27th Street, which belonged to the Union of Jewish Cooperative Societies in Warsaw. There were 285 registered Jewish commercial and manufacturing establishments, and 103 Jewish craft workshops in 1939. Jewish merchants and craftsmen had a Union of Jewish Merchants and a Union of Jewish Artisans.

The Jewish community was not particularly wealthy. Of almost 600 persons who paid membership dues to the community in 1938, only eight had incomes in excess of 30,000 złoty. The incomes of 304 people, on the other hand, were less than 2,500 złoty. If we remember that the family of the average Jewish taxpayer numbered 4.7 persons, then we see that they lived in rather modest circumstances.

Zionism

Several Zionist organizations and Jewish political parties were active in Poznań. They included the General Zionist Organization, the Union of Revisionist Zionists, Poale Zion (the Jewish Socialist Workers' Party), the Bund and the Agudas (the Orthodox grouping).

The first of these, the General Zionist Organization, had arisen as a political party after the 1917 Balfour Declaration in which the British government committed itself to the creation of a Jewish national home in Palestine. Its goals were the inculcation of the Zionist ideology and the collection of donations to Keren Kayemet (the Jewish national fund, used for the purchase of land in Palestine) and Keren Hayesot (a fund for the support of settlers in Palestine). The organization was supported by the separate but coordinated youth movements, Hashomer Hatzair (Young Scouts) and Hehalutz Hamerkazi (Central Pioneers).

The former of these groups was unusually popular among the Jewish youth of Poznań, who were attracted by its scouting character and uniforms. Hashomer Hatzair members included students from the upper grades of primary school through to post-secondary school. They were divided into groups whose leaders conducted lessons in the geography of Palestine, Jewish history, the Hebrew language, scouting lore and sports training. They took part in Lag Ba-Omer outings to celebrate Bar Kochba's successes against the Romans. Hashomer Hatzair organized training sessions, attended by young people from Poznań, until the outbreak of the war, for settlement and work in Palestine. There were also summer camps supervised by Hashomer instructors.

The Union of Revisionist Zionists was opposed to the General Zionists and the workers' parties. Its extremist politics called for a ruthless struggle against the Arabs and against the proletarian Histadrut movement. The leader of the party was Vladimir Jabotinsky, who came to Poznań to give speeches.

The Jewish Socialist Workers' Party was the right-wing faction of the Poale Zion party, which had existed since 1905. The strongest working-class party in Poland, however, was the Bund, the General Jewish Workers' Union. Its main goal was the replacement of the capitalist system with a socialist one. Neither the Bund not the Orthodox Agudas movement enjoyed much support in Poznań.

There were also two small Jewish Masonic lodges in Poznań. The Amicitia Lodge, at 5 Stawna Street, was part of the B'nai B'rith (Sons of the Covenant) order. The second lodge, known as the Kosmos Lodge, had its headquarters on

Marcinkowski Avenue. Both lodges were liquidated as a result
of the 22 November 1938 decree by the president of the Polish
Republic.

Education

Before the beginning of the 1919–20 school year, the Polish
authorities approved a proposal from the Jewish School
Association to open a primary school for Jewish children. The
school began operating on 1 May 1919, in a private house on
Małe Garbary Street. Shortly afterwards it was relocated to a
building at the corner of Szewska and Stawna Streets. In the
first year, 71 children attended. Some of them also went to
other primary schools at the same time. A new school at 3
Noskowski Street was opened in 1932. Primary School 14, for
Jewish children, was located here until the beginning of the
war. It had seven grades, and the principal was Mrs
Franciszka Propst. More than 200 children attended each year.
There was a school shelter for children from the poorest families and meals were served in the winter months. There was
also a Jewish kindergarten at 5 Szewska Street.

At the secondary level, young people attended *gymnazjum*.
Some went to the Schiller German *gymnazjum*, and others to
the popular school known as the 'Paderek'. There was such a
demand for secondary education that in 1937 the Judischer
Schulverein applied to the regional educational authority for
permission to open a Jewish *gymnazjum* in Poznań. There
were many Jewish students at the University of Poznań, especially in the faculties of medicine and mathematics and natural sciences. Some of them belonged to the local chapter of
Dror, the Zionist Revisionist students' organization.

A Jewish religious school (*cheder*) occupied premises in the
Jewish community building at 10 Szewska Street. There were
classes in both Yiddish and Hebrew. However, the fact that it
did not offer instruction in secular subjects meant that its
pupils had to attend another school as well.

The S.L. Peretz Jewish Popular Library Association carried
on educational activities. The chairman of the board was
Benjamin Goldberg. There were also libraries on Szewska

Street and at the Foundation Home for the Elderly on
Żydowska Street.

Pojzner Sztyme (The Voice of Poznań), a weekly newspaper,
began to appear in 1935. Its editorial offices were at 16
Wroniecka Street and it was printed (two pages in Polish and
four in Yiddish) in Kalisz.

There was also a Bar Kochba sports club. Its most active
section was the boxing team.

The anti-Jewish press

The publishers of the chauvinistic and nationalistic, anti-
Jewish press operated freely in prewar Poznań. One of the
most fervent was *Głos Ojczyzny* (The Voice of the Fatherland),
a biweekly founded in 1924 by Mieczysław Noskowicz, president of the board of directors of the anti-Jewish League for the
Defence of the Fatherland and the Faith. Before it ceased publication in 1929, the newspaper accepted advertising only
from Christian merchants.

Rozwój (Development) was the name of the Union for
Social Self-Defence. In 1927, the Union began publishing a
monthly magazine that was commonly referred to as 'The
Black Book'. It listed the names of the customers of Jewish
shops. Other anti-Semitic titles in the 1930s included *Under the
Magnifying Glass* ['Pod preqięvz'], *The Spider* ['Pająk'] and
National Self-Defence ['Samoobrona navodu'].

The struggle against the 'Jewish deluge' was also carried
on by the National Democrat press, and especially the *Kurier
Poznański* (Poznań Courier), which in the 1920s was still
publishing rumours about the ritual use of Christian blood.
The most common stereotypes in the press were those of the
Jewish communist, the Jewish banker, and the international
financier. The weekly *Rozwój*, published by the above-
mentioned organization (which had branches in Poznań and
throughout Wielkopolska), enjoyed considerable popularity.
As early as 1922, it faced a slander prosecution for a poster
showing a Pole driving Jewish-looking rats out of a barn. The
Poznań branch of the Catholic St Joseph's Artisans' Society fell
under the influence of *Rozwój*.

The outbreak of war

Before the arrival of German troops early in September 1939, many Jewish people from Poznań travelled eastward to other places in Poland where they had relatives. Those who remained behind waited to see how things would turn out. The Germans marched into the city on 10 September. Five days later they confiscated all of the thousand books in the Jewish library. They forbade Jewish schools to open on 16 September, and ordered Jewish shops to close on the 20th. These shops were to be taken over by the NSV (National Socialist Social Welfare) organization. On 20 October the first Jewish victims, Benno Rindfleisch and Juliusz Tychauer, were shot at Fort VII. Several more Jews were shot in the same month, in Poznań and in the localities of Buk and Kórnik.

A resettlement camp for Poles was opened on Bałtycka Street in the central district on 5 November. A week later, SS-Gruppenführer Koppe, the Supreme Commander of the SS and police in the Warthe Land, issued instructions for the resettlement of all Jews and 35,000 Poles. More Jews were shot at Fort VII. From 29 November, the Jews of Poznań were required to wear the Star of David on their chests and a yellow armband on their sleeves. On 11 December the Gestapo ordered the Jewish community to organize the assembly of all the city's Jewish residents on Bałtycka Street at eight o'clock the following morning. They were placed in a barrack and had their baggage taken away. The following day, approximately 1,500 Jewish people were taken on trains to the General Government for resettlement. The majority were deported to Ostrów Lubelski. Many later found themselves in the Warsaw and Łódź ghettos. The majority died in the Treblinka, Chełmno and Auschwitz death camps.

Seven days after the deportation, the trust office finished the work of confiscating Jewish shops. The following morning, 20 December, Dr Friemart drove to Dziekanka near Gniezno, where he supervised the euthanasia killing of the Jewish and Polish patients at the mental hospital.

Work began on the conversion of the Stawna Street synagogue into a swimming pool. On 15 April 1940, the Germans ceremonially removed the last Star of David from the building. The Poznań Jewish district had ceased to exist.

Labour camps

The majority of the Jewish population of the Poznań occupation zone had been deported by the end of February 1940. In March, however, the Reich authorities suspended their deportation plans because of the need for labourers. The first, and central, Jewish labour camp in Poznań was set up in the buildings attached to the Municipal Stadium on Dolna Wilda Street. It went into operation in the spring of 1941. At any given time, there were about a thousand Jews there. They had been arrested, expelled from their homes, or caught during street round-ups. They were used as labour in public works, construction, gardening and transport throughout the city. Most of them had to sleep outdoors in appalling conditions. There was terror, starvation and disease. Apart from the Municipal Stadium, there were also over 20 camps in Poznań: for example, in Antoninek, Dębiec, Franowo, Golęcin, Żabikowo, Kobylempole, Krzesiny, Krzesinki, Krzyżowniki, Malta, Piotrowo, Smochowice and Strzeszyn after the liquidation of the main camp in early 1943, the prisoners were transferred to the camp in Krzesiny– Piotrowo. At the end of 1943 there were still some four to five thousand Jewish prisoners there.

Jews were also held in a camp in Żabikowo. About 300 people, working on the construction of the Frankfurt–Poznań–Łódź *autobahn*, were there in 1941 and 1942. They also laboured, after November 1942, at preparing the grounds and barracks of a camp for political prisoners in Żabikowo.

The committee on Żydowska Street

Those who survived the war returned afterwards to their home towns. In the case of Poznań, those who returned were individuals, for only a few dozen of the city's Jewish residents survived. At times, they only stayed for a few hours or days, in hope that relatives or friends may have survived, or left word as to their whereabouts. The situation was made more complicated by the fact that survivors could not go back to their old homes, which had been taken over by new owners. The only way to recover their property was through the courts.

The majority of the Jews of Poznań had perished in the ghettos and concentration camps of Chełmno, Treblinka and Auschwitz. The survivors were, in most cases, those who had spent the war in Soviet territory. A few others had been liberated from concentration camps in Germany. Only one case is known of a Jew who survived the war in hiding in Poznań.

Nevertheless, a handful of Jewish former residents came back in 1945 and 1946. They needed assistance, and a branch of the Central Committee of Jews in Poland (CKŻP) was set up. It was located in the former old people's home on Żydowska Street. Committee employees wrote letters, attempted to locate relatives, and distributed aid sent by JOINT (Jewish American Joint Distribution Committee).

Jews also returned to other cities in Wielkopolska. For instance, 2,200 returned to Kalisz. This was the largest centre of Jewry in the province. Before the war, 25,000 Jews had lived there. While only five natives of Kalisz survived from the whole Łódź ghetto, it was possible to live out the war in the Soviet Union. Whole families returned: the Frenkls (six people), the Szmerlings (11), the Bessers (six). Other Jews had survived with partisan units or in the army.

Many Jews from Kalisz, Poznań, Konin, and other towns in the Wielkopolska region settled after the war in Lower Silesia, Szczecin, or Łódź. Others had joined General Anders' army and travelled with it to the Near East. Some of the Jewish people who were liberated from camps in Germany went straight off to join relatives in England, France, the United States, Canada or Australia, without ever returning to Poland.

One of the main issues for the Jewish people who returned to Poland and the Wielkopolska region was the question of personal safety. Anti-Semitism and nationalism remained alive despite the Holocaust, and Poles who had sheltered Jews during the war were sometimes afraid to admit to their neighbours afterwards that they had done so. Historians estimate that nearly 2,000 Jewish people were murdered in liberated Poland between 1944 and 1947. There were also pogroms, the most notorious of which occurred in Kielce, Cracow and Parczewo. The dangerous atmosphere inclined most Jews to think of leaving Poland. Some travelled to the Displaced Persons' camps in Germany. Brich, the Zionist

Coordinating organization, dealt with mass emigration to Palestine. Brich posts were set up in Szczecin, Żary and Zgorzelec in the west, and at Wałbrzych and Kudowa in the south of Poland. The Central Committee of Jews in Poland had its own emigration office which, however, worked very sluggishly. The Hebrew Immigrant Aid Society (HIAS), familiar from before the war, and the PAL-Amt organization both began operating in 1946. The Jews who emigrated from Poznań and Wielkopolska usually did so by semi-legal routes.

After 1948 it became increasingly difficult to leave Poland. People who submitted petitions to emigrate usually received in reply forms to be filled out. These forms were in fact declarations that they had renounced the idea of leaving. The borders reopened in 1956. The last cases of emigration from Poznań are noted in 1967–68. Among these was the world renowned sociologist, Professor Zygmunt Bauman.

The gravestones cry out

Several gravestones, transferred to the Miłostów cemetery, are all that remains of the Jews of Poznań. The former synagogue, converted during the war into a swimming pool, still stands in the centre of town, as does the building on Żydowska Street that contained the Jewish old people's home, the Bet Midrash and the apartment in which the last rabbi of Poznań resided. Other buildings belonging to the Jewish community are also left. Some vestiges of the former inhabitants can still be found in the Żabikowo museum and in the library collections. There is nothing more. There is not a single street in Poznań named after any Jewish resident of the city. There are no memorial plaques on the synagogue, the Jewish school, or the other buildings that still recall a multi-cultural Poznań.

Yet the Jews lived here for more than 800 years. They worked among the Poles and the Germans. They sold their merchandise, treated all patients without regard to faith or ethnic origins, and they prayed in the synagogue on Stawna Street after the death of Marshal Piłsudski. When all is said and done, they worshipped the same God as the Catholics and the protestants. They were born here and they died here.

21

There were periods when every third resident of Poznań was Jewish, and when the Jewish community of the city ranked among the most important and wealthiest in Poland. It is worth remembering all of this in the face of the fact that the Poznań Jewish community was quite small in the years before the Second World War. The history of the town did not begin in 1918. Today, therefore, a place must be found for the memory of those who so loved this city, for the memory of the Jews for whom Poznań was their 'first' home town.

PART I

Who Saves One Life …

1 The Righteous

Corporal Władysław Głowacki became a priest in 1929. He had graduated earlier from the Railroad and Technical Enlisted Men's Military School in Poznań. He was thirty-eight when the war began. He found himself in the Warsaw ghetto in October 1940. He became the prefect of the Church of the Most Blessed Virgin Mary at 34 Leszno Street.

We read in Ringelblum's *Chronicle*[1] that, apart from Father Głowacki, there were approximately 1,540 Roman Catholics living in the ghetto in January 1941. There were also 148 Lutherans, 30 Eastern Orthodox Christians and 43 people who professed other non-Jewish faiths. Ringelblum writes about people who were baptized in the ghetto. Nineteen people converted to Catholicism and one to Orthodoxy in the month of June 1940 alone. In his diary, Professor Ludwik Hirszfeld[2] asks, 'What motive can these people have?' He answers his own question: 'They had nothing to gain. The change in faith did not alter their legal status in the least. They were not attracted by the charms of the religion of love. The religion professed by the nation to which they regarded themselves as belonging. A religion in which there is not, or at least is not supposed to be, any place for hatred. How worn down these Jews are by the atmosphere of general indifference. For what?'

Marian Fuks, in turn, writes in his foreword to the Diary of Adam Czerniakow[3] that some naïve Jews believed that conversion could save their lives. 'These baptisms, of course, turned out to be useless,' Fuks writes, 'and they caused the converts nothing but trouble.' In the Orthodox Jewish Community, for instance, officials attempted to deprive converted Jews of their rights and of whatever aid was available. A list of '*mehes*' (converts) was drawn up, and they were excluded from all 'privileges'. Czerniakow did not approve of such a step. When charged with tolerating converts, he replied: 'The ghetto is not a Jewish state. It is a place where converted Jews also live, and that is why they deserve equal treatment.'

There were two parishes, two churches, within the 'closed district'. The parish priest of All Saints was Monsignor Marceli Godlewski, and Jewish intellectuals lived in the rectory along with the priests. One of them was Professor Ludwik Hirszfeld, with his family.

Father Tadeusz Puder, a priest of Jewish ethnic background, was the parish priest at the church on Leszno Street. It was here that Father Władysław Głowacki, the corporal from Poznań, served as prefect from October 1940 to August 1942. Under the date of 25 December 1941, Ringelblum notes in his *Chronicle* that a crowd of simple, devout people attended that church.

On 14 June 1942, Jechiel Górny – a member of the staff of the Ghetto Archive and a future soldier in the Jewish Combat Organization (ŻOB) – wrote in his Diary:

Through the open window comes the sound of the organ. A service is underway in the church on Leszno Street (the churchyard abuts on my building at 23 Nowolipie). How much this view means within the walls of the ghetto: several trees in blossom, ploughed earth, green grass. Groups of well-dressed people are strolling there, the men in dark suits and the women in elegant dresses, and among them a tall figure in a black cassock ...

Dusk falls slowly: first the faces, and then the figures of the people disappear in the darkness but – what an irony! – the white armbands with the Star of David are visible from afar like patches on their right sleeves. What a twist of fate it is that those people, who abandoned the Jews for various reasons, have now been cast back whence they came, by the barbarians of the twentieth century. Many of them, especially among the young, did not even know that their ancestors were Jewish. . . . There is some sort of special ceremony in the church on Leszno Street today, perhaps a wedding ... The sounds of the hymns grow quieter. Quietly, in muffled voices barely audibly in the silence of the June evening, they are singing *Boże, coś Polskę* [a Polish patriotic hymn].

That tall figure in the black cassock could well have been Father Głowacki. Jechiel Górny does not say. It is known, however, that Father Władysław aided Jews by issuing false baptismal certificates. Amelia and Rudolf Areichowski, Aleksander Bender and Maksymilian Seidenbeutel benefited from his efforts. At the time of the first liquidation operation in June, Głowacki was transferred to the parish in Służewic. There, he cooperated with the Resistance and continued to help people from the ghetto. A Jewish woman, Helena Łabędź, was in hiding at his rectory from August 1942 until the end of the war.

Henryk Krüger was born in Poznań. When the war broke out, he was living in Warsaw. He was in commerce, and he helped Jewish acquaintances from the time when the ghetto was set up. Those he aided included an engineer named Brühl, who lived on Jaworzyńska Street and had been in the wholesale lumber business before the war. Brühl found himself in difficulties when his bank account was frozen after the Germans took Warsaw. Krüger helped him until mid 1940. When a *volksdeutsch* named Glappy moved into Brühl's apartment, Krüger lost touch with the lumber merchant. Brühl probably ended up in the ghetto.

After the closed district had been established, Krüger supplied Halina Wald with food. Halina was twenty then and lived on Orła Street. Minna Frydland lived with her parents on Franciszkańska Street. Krüger helped her as well. On 22 July 1942, the first day of the mass deportation to Treblinka, Minna sent word to Krüger that she was in trouble and asked him to come to the Court Building on Leszno Street. Guessing what her message meant, he took a false identity card, made out to 'Wanda Mak', to the agreed place. He led the girl down

27

Biała Street and over to the Aryan side, where he had an apartment prepared for her. When extortionists took an interest in the girl, Krüger had to ransom her, find her somewhere else to live, and fit her out with a new identity card. Minna lived at 15 Marszałkowska Street under the name of Maria Burzyńska, and she had a baptismal certificate from the Church of the Holy Cross in Warsaw. After the suppression of the Warsaw Uprising, she was deported to Germany as a forced labourer. She went to Canada after the war. Halina Wald also survived the occupation. After living in France for a time, she too moved to Canada.

On 25 November 1976, Minna Frydland Aspler sent a deposition to Yad Vashem in which she wrote:

While we were in the ghetto, Mr Krüger helped me and my family. Afterwards, he helped me to escape to the Aryan side, found me a safe hiding place, and ransomed me from the clutches of Gestapo agents after I was denounced. From that time on, Krüger himself had to go into hiding. He could not work, and his only source of support consisted of donations that we received from underground organizations.

Edmund Łuczak graduated from the Poznań University Medical School in 1937. He began serving an internship at a hospital in Kalisz. He was drafted into the army in September 1939. He was in Warsaw when it was under siege. After the Germans took the capital, he moved to Lisków, near Kalisz. He took up a post in the local orphanage and resumed his medical career.

A woman named Landau escaped in late 1942 from a transport on its way to the death camp at Chełmno on the Ner (Kulmhof). She escaped along with her 13-year-old daughter, Natalia. They said that they came from Uniejów. At first, they hid in the woods. When her mother died, Natalia took shelter with a peasant named Krych in the village of Żydowo, near Lisków. Natalia's leg was injured. There was a danger of gangrene. Doctor Łuczak, knowing that she was a Jewish child, treated her. Natalia recovered thanks to his care. This was one of many cases in which the physician from Lisków rendered medical aid to Jews. Many years later, Natalia traced Dr

Łuczak. She wrote that her name was now Rachelle Nelkin, and that she lived in England. She thanked him for saving her life and wrote to Yad Vashem to nominate him for the 'Righteous Among the Nations' medal.

Krystyna Meringe was deported from Poznań during the occupation. She and her parents, Zofia and Witold, were assigned to a country estate called Zuzanka, near Warsaw. In 1941, she met Tadeusz Grostal there. From the day they met, she began helping Grostal and his family. Until the deportation from the ghetto, she took food to Tadeusz's father, Jakub. After the deportation, she could not locate Jakub. He probably died in Treblinka. Krystyna also looked after Tadeusz's mother, Sabina Grostal, who was in hiding at Milanówek. Additionally, she aided Tadeusz's aunt, Justyna Grostal Kalina, wife of the linguist Paweł Kalina, who was the author of several dictionaries.

In 1942 Krystyna Meringe and Tadeusz Grostal were married. They travelled to Zakopane. Under the name 'Teodor Hanke', Tadeusz found employment with the town council there. When he was denounced, he escaped from the Gestapo and fled to Warsaw. He obtained a new identity card and underwent plastic surgery at the Omega clinic. He survived the war thanks to the help of Krystyna Meringe.

Maria Suszczewicz lived in Konarzewo, near Poznań, before the war and during the occupation. Henryka and Henryk Goldman lived in Sosnowiec. Their daughter Zosia was born in September 1939. When it was confirmed that the ghetto in Sosnowiec was to be liquidated, an acquaintance of the Goldmans took the child to Poznań. Maria Suszczewicz was waiting on the platform for little Zosia. She took her home to Konarzewo. At times of heightened danger, the child stayed with Maria Rowińska in Wronki.

When the war ended, Zosia's father, Henryk Goldman, came to Konarzewo. Fate carried the little girl to far-away

Australia. From there, as Naomi Goldrei, she corresponded with Maria Suszczewicz, a 'Righteous' woman from Konarzewo.

The Tęgi family had a shoe store in Kościano. When the war broke out, 31-year-old Stanisław was drafted into the army. He was taken prisoner after the Polish defeat in September 1939. He managed to escape from the prisoner-of-war camp at Biedruskol, near Poznań, in October. He returned to Kościan. Soon afterwards, fearing that the Germans were looking for him, he went to Warsaw. His wife and children joined him there.

Stanisław Tęgi opened a shop selling luggage at 33 Chmielna Street in Warsaw. Jerzy Pfeffer, who had managed to escape from the Majdanek death camp, knocked on his door in 1943. Tęgi helped him. He gave him clothing, money and, for a time, shelter in the back room of the shop.

Stanisław Tęgi and his wife Irena both died in 1984. Not until 5 May 1986, did Jerzy Pfeffer write to Yad Vashem. He stated: 'Stanisław Tęgi frequently sheltered me in a room adjacent to his shop on Chmielna Street in Warsaw. He helped me financially and supplied me with underclothing and clothing, and helped me to obtain a loan of a thousand dollars from a friend of his. Thanks to that money, I lived a year in hiding at Mrs Żelichowska's.'

Roman Ratomski, a prominent Poznań orthopaedist, was a small boy, full of vigour and the desire for a normal life, at the time of the war. He lived then in Warsaw, on Puławska Street, with his mother Emilia. His father, an air force colonel, had been abroad in the diplomatic service since 1935. When the war began, he held a post in Moscow.

As the predicament of the Jews of Warsaw worsened, Emilia Ratomska's school friend, Ludwika Oberleider, called on her. She asked for help. 'Without a moment's hesitation,' Roman Ratomski recalled, 'my mother took Ludwika in.

Overnight, we had three Jewish women, Ludwika, her mother and her sister, living in our apartment.' Two weeks later, fearing denunciation to the Gestapo, Emilia Ratomska found them a new apartment in the Żolibórz district. The women, however, were blackmailed by extortionists there, and returned to Puławska Street. From there, Mrs Ratomska settled them in Milanówek. She found them another apartment and more people who would be able to help them. She found them jobs, identity cards and money. Her son Roman helped. They also found a place for other Jews to stay in Milanówek. They managed to help some 30 people. They took them to church and taught them how to pray and to pretend to be Catholics.

When Ludwika Haren visited Poland in 1991, she was unable to meet Emilia Ratomska, who had died. However, she informed Emilia's son that the survivors had applied to Yad Vashem so that they could receive the 'Righteous Among the Nations' medal. Roman Ratomski could not wait for the medal to arrive in Poland. When he heard that the nomination had been approved, he got on a plane to Israel. He went to Yad Vashem in order to receive the medal personally from the director, Mordechai Paldiel. Ludwika Haren stood beside him. Roman Ratomski returned to Poland as quickly as he could. Although his mother was no longer alive, he wanted to go to her grave as soon as possible to read out that special sentence engraved on the medal: 'Who saves one life, saves the whole world.'

NOTES

1. Emanuel Ringelblum was a famous freedom fighter and the historian and chronicler of the Warsaw Ghetto. The Ringelblum Archive was hidden in Pawiak Prison.
2. Professor Ludwik Hirszfeld (1884–1954) was a bacteriologist, whose family managed to escape from the Warsaw ghetto just before the final liquidation. There is now the Ludwik Hirszfeld Institute of Immunology and Experimental Therapy in Wroclaw, Poland.
3. Adam Czerniakow served as chairman of the Judenrat in the Warsaw ghetto for nearly three years. The Center for Advanced Holocaust Studies has published his diary, *Prelude to Doom: The Warsaw Diary of Adam Czerniakow*, R. Hilberg, S. Staron and J. Kermisz (eds) (trans. S. Staron and staff of Yad Vashem) (The Center for Advanced Holocaust Studies Academic Publications, 1999).

2 More Dust

Helena Szczepaniak, whose maiden name was Pawlaczyk, lives near Corpus Christi Church in Poznań. She received a letter from Cipora and Taube one day. The Frenkiel sisters wrote: 'We have requested that Yad Vashem award you and your sister Zosia the "Righteous Among the Nations of the World" medal.' Several months passed. Taube Frenkiel died in Canada, and Zosia Pawlaczyk died in Poznań. They both died in the same year: 1992. Then two more years went by. The ambassador of Israel came to Poznań. There were medals for both sisters, but only one sister to receive them. It was a gloomy November day. 'The mood that accompanied the reception of the medals,' Helena Szczepaniak recalls, 'was reminiscent of falling leaves. Full of melancholy, tears and bitterness.'

Helena was fourteen when the war began. She remembers the first of September well. That was the day when she was supposed to start attending her new school. She was proud of herself for having been accepted at the Commercial *Gymnazjum* on Sniadeckich Street. Morning fog hung over the city. Police in helmets patrolled the streets. Dozens of people who wanted to leave town were on their way to the Poznań railroad station. The first air raid alarm sounded at 8.30. And so, instead of sitting at a desk in her new school, Helena had to run downstairs to hide in the cellar from attacks by German bombers. The all-clear soon sounded. In her memoirs, however, Helena Szczepaniak wrote, 'All my dreams burst.' Years later, she also recalls the sarcastic contrariness of the time when the word 'homeland' stopped being an abstraction, and joy over the death of an enemy became a fact. It was precisely the latter experience that was completely new. The enemy, she told herself, was also a person. And she could never bring herself to accept what she witnessed on Kraszewski Street.

'It happened before the German army entered Poznań,' she recalls. 'I was walking down Kraszewskiego. Suddenly I noticed a group of boy scouts wearing red-and-white armbands. They were leading a German woman, the owner of a shop with wicker goods, out into the street. She was sobbing and squirming between the two strapping boys who held her by the arms, pushing her and dragging her along. Every few steps, she dug in her heels and cried out, "Gentlemen, have mercy! I'm no spy!" But the passersby shouted: "String up the spy on a lamp post." I saw how one of the scouts gave the weeping woman a series of blows across the back with a stick. It turned out that a pile of German newspapers had been found in her shop and in the adjoining apartment. But the newspaper was the *Posener Tageblatt*, which was published under Polish auspices in Poznań. A picture of Hitler, some newspaper clippings on NSDAP successes, and a flag with a swastika had also been found.

I still remember that procession. The terrified woman was being led along by the boys and by onlookers shouting, "Burn the spy's newspapers in front of her shop!" Something inside me was touched. I felt sickened by the spectacle. I was fourteen. I did not know what "the fifth column" was. I knew nothing about the problems of national minorities.

In the autumn of 1940 Helena was sent to an ammunition factory in Lübeck. The new female workers were given pea soup. That was the first time in her life that she saw a piece of bacon complete with the skin and hair of the pig in her soup dish. She pushed the dish away and ran outside. 'I never had that at home,' she told her new fellow-workers. Soon, however, she would experience the taste of hunger. A year later, she escaped from Lübeck to Poznań. It was unbearable at home. She never went out for fear of being recognized. At the end of February, she made up her mind to go back to Lübeck. When the foreman saw her, he looked at her as if she were some sort of exotic bird. Several months passed and she received a letter from her sister in Poznań. Zosia wrote: 'I have a job and money to buy food with.' That must have been about the time that a fellow employee called Truda informed her that she was taking a legal leave of absence in connection with her mother's illness.'I'm going with you,' Helena decided on the spot. So she sneaked away from Lübeck a second time. The journey to Poznań took many hours. When she walked in the door, her younger sister Łucja exclaimed in terror, 'O my God! It's Helena's ghost! Something must have happened!'

She could not stay in Poznań, so she and Zosia decided to go to Warsaw, where their good friend Ruta lived. Ruta promised to take care of them. They set out by train in the direction of Katowice. Someone was supposed to smuggle them across the border into the General Government near Trzebinia. They crossed over at dawn – Helena remembers how the birds were singing. In her diary she wrote: 'My heart was pounding and I squeezed Zosia's hand.' On Friday, 4 September, they reached Warsaw.

That same day, there was an unusually strict search of the workshops in the Warsaw ghetto. SS men, accompanied by Ukrainians and Latvians, took 1,669 people to Umschlagplatz for 'resettlement'. This was the first act of the final great resettlement operation, from the ghetto to the Treblinka death camp. The so-called 'registration' began on Sunday, 6 September. All the Jews who remained alive were ordered to assemble in the area bounded by Gęsia, Zamenhofa, Lubecki and Stawki Streets. Each German firm was assigned a quota of workers. The lucky people got numbers. 'Numbers meant life,' Marek Edelman recalled. Nothing mattered anymore except obtaining a number. Those who had no number were led to Umschlagplatz

In the course of a week, from 6 to 12 September, 50,000 Jews were dispatched to Treblinka. Women with children had the worst prospects for surviving the registration. Sometimes men managed to save children in sacks. It worked like this: a father threw a sack containing his child on to his back, gave a bribe to the Ukrainian sentry, and carried the child out. Many Jews were dying then of hunger and thirst, and were afraid to come out of their hiding places even when their food supplies ran out. The streets were full of corpses. Food prices rose. A kilogram of bread cost 100 złoty, a kilo of potatoes 50 złoty.

Living was cheaper on the Aryan side. The last deportation from the ghetto took place on 21 September, Yom Kippur. That day 2,196 people were sent to Treblinka, and the area of the ghetto was radically reduced. We read in a report sent to the Polish government-in-exile in London: 'The Jews are reeling psychologically … . The curtain of death is slowly descending upon the Jewry of Warsaw.'

At first, Helena and Zosia stayed with Ruta, then after a few days they rented a room on Bonifraterska Street, literally a few steps from the ghetto. That was when they met the Frenkiels, a Jewish family. They met Szyja first, and then Taube – or rather, Kazik and Wanda. Kazik and Wanda were living on the Aryan side. Their parents, Miriam and Szepsel, were living in the ghetto, as were their twin siblings, Cypora and Zaumenys (or rather Celinka and Zyga). Kazik was living on Bonifraterska Street under the name 'Kazimierz Lisowski', and Wanda's name was Irena Lisowska. She was afraid that she would be recognized by her father's old customers, because she had worked as a sales clerk in the leather goods store that her father had run before the war. Furthermore, she had very Semitic-looking facial features. For this reason, she changed her name four times during the war. Kazik, for his part, underwent a foreskin operation. He was a handsome 27-year-old man with blue eyes and an Aryan appearance; so he could move freely about Warsaw. He told the Pawlaczyk sisters about what was happening in the ghetto. He told them about the 300,000 people who had been killed or sent to Treblinka in the big deportation operation.

The Polish police came one day in December. Fortunately, the sisters were alone. The police said that Jews were hiding in the apartment. The girls denied this. In the course of the conversation, they said that their father was also a policeman and was then in an internment camp in Hungary. The policemen became more amicable, and even offered to help the girls find jobs.

Kazik wanted to be in more frequent contact with his family. He arranged for Helena to obtain a pass and a job in the ghetto. This enabled her to go to the Frenkiels' apartment. That was when she understood what it was that made the ghetto so horrible. She saw Germans shooting children, contraband artists making grand fortunes, and food smugglers paying with their lives for a hunk of bread. She saw human corpses lying in the streets until the sanitation service collected them. She learned about the ghastly scenes at Umschlagplatz. Most of the Jews were employed in workshops. Their food ration consisted of watery soup and a quarter pound of bread. They had to wear their numbers as a sign that they had legal employment – without numbers they were shot on the spot. The people who were alive acted as if they were under a death sentence, waiting only for the date of their execution to be fixed.

Kazik and Zosia became very close, and eventually he proposed. Helena kept going into the ghetto. Once, she saw a little boy returning from the Aryan side with a couple of carrots in his hand. He was lucky: he got off with a beating from a Jewish policeman that left him bleeding. Helen found the workshop where Szepsel Frankiel worked. She told him that a hiding place was ready for his family on Krochmalna Street. She took him money and jewellery, which she usually concealed under her garter belt or in a secret pouch in her purse. When she entered the workshop, little Zyga Frenkiel would run up to her. As they were walking along the street one day, little Zyga asked, 'Tell me, Helena, is the sunshine as sad on the other side of the wall as it is in the ghetto?' She told him that the sunshine was the same on both sides of the wall. 'But here in the ghetto, she said, there is more dust, and that is what makes the sun seem so pale and sad.'

Apart from their apartment on Bonifraterska Street, the Pawlaczyks rented a place on Żółkiewski Street. Many Jews passed through both apartments in their quest for rescue. One of them was Lilianna Goldwobel, who survived the war and emigrated to Canada in 1952. On one occasion, Kazik brought a Jewish acquaintance of his, Zygmunt Malewski, to the apartment on Żółkiewski Street, where he underwent a foreskin operation. Zygmunt survived the war, but died soon afterwards in a motorcycle accident.

Things were getting worse and worse in the ghetto. The district was sealed off on 18 January. The second liquidation operation was beginning. Now, for the first time, the Germans encountered resistance. The fighting began at the intersection of Miła and Zamenhofa Streets. But the ŻOB, the Jewish Combat Organization, had too few weapons for a straight fight. The losses were heavy, so they went over to guerrilla fighting. One guerrilla group was surrounded by the Germans before weapons could be supplied to it, and was led to Umschlagplatz. When the 60 young fighters were ordered into the railway carriage, their commander, Pelc, delivered a fiery oration. They refused to get in. The head of the Treblinka camp shot them all on the spot.

The situation was getting worse and worse. Everyone knew that the Germans would soon initiate the final liquidation of the ghetto. It was decided that Ruta would make her way through the sewers to the Frenkiels, in order to make detailed arrangements for getting them out to the Aryan side. It was 21 February 1943. Ruta was lucky enough to make it back. She brought little Celina along. She registered the little girl to live with her, and made out that she was the daughter of a brother-in-law who lived in France. Helena spent hours teaching Celina how to say the rosary. 'If the police catch you,' Helena told her, 'you'd better know how to cross yourself.' The news coming out of the ghetto was increasingly dire. It became impossible to get the Frenkiels out, as even the manholes into the sewers were under guard. Then the uprising broke out and Miriam Frenkiel died in her burning home. Her husband died of a heart attack. The Germans took 13-year-old Zygmunt to Majdanek.

The uprising was almost over. Helena remembers how the Gestapo came to Bonifraterska Street on 17 May and took away Romek, who had been smuggled out of the ghetto by Kazik. Romek had impeccable papers, and had been planning for several weeks to join a partisan group, yet he could not break away from the ghetto. The Gestapo finally caught him. They ordered him to drop his trousers. Zosia saw how they shot him on the street. The apartment was 'burned'. When Ruta, Kazik and Celina returned home the next day, the janitor warned them about the raid. The police came back to confiscate property brought out of the ghetto.

New papers were made for Wanda. She lived in Poznań for a while, and later on Zielona Street in Warsaw. Kazik was arrested in Poznań in March 1944 and imprisoned in Fort VII. Later, he was transferred to Warsaw and then to Stutthof Concentration Camp, where, pretending to be an Aryan, he survived.

Szyja Frenkiel emigrated to Canada after the war. Helena Szczepaniak does not want to talk about it. Kazik abandoned her sister. He (supposedly) fell in love with a German woman. Is this possible? It was with the German woman that he crossed the ocean, and it was the German woman who became his wife.

Helena still remembers the charred scraps of paper and clothing that were borne on the wind. For her, clouds of dark smoke still hang over the ghetto. If you opened the window for only a moment, you were covered in soot. But could she have gone on living behind a closed window, without that clinging soot in her hair?

3 A Human Reaction

Rzepecki heard a knocking at the door. Józef Mandelman, a one-legged Jewish man, was standing there. 'Bronisław, help me. I don't want to go on living,' Józef said, and broke down crying. 'You could go to the pharmacy in Stopnica,' he said. 'They'll sell you poison. The pharmacist knows you. I can't leave Oleśnica. Besides, who would sell poison to a Jew?'

Rzepecki refused. 'I'd have your life on my conscience,' he explained to the terrified Mandelman, and asked, 'How could I live with that?' Rzepecki knew that Mandelman had no chance at all of surviving. The Germans shot people like him on the spot. What could be done? 'If I leave him standing out there and don't help him, I'll have that on my conscience, too,' he thought, as he looked at the desperate man.

Fifty years later, Rzepecki remembers every detail from the day when Mandelman knocked on his door. He had to make up his mind. 'I was well aware,' he says, as we sit in his Poznań apartment, 'that aiding Jews was punishable by death. I knew that any humane reaction would also expose my family to the risk of death.'

Could he leave Mandelman standing outside the door to face certain extermination? Could he allow Mandelman's children to watch their father being murdered on the main square in Oleśnica? It took only a second to make the decision: 'We might be able to shelter your family at Krawczyk's farm.' Stanisław Krawczyk's farmyard stood in the middle of the fields, well back from the road. They dug a cellar under the barn. That was the hiding place for Józef and Anna Mandelman, their son Abraham, their daughters Tamara and Rut, and Mandelman's two sons-in-law.

Only a few Jewish families lived in Oleśnica before the war. There were a couple of shopkeepers, a baker and a butcher whose daughter sold meat door-to-door. They had lived there for generations. People said, 'These are our Jews.' Rzepecki cannot recall any conflicts. The Jews had a prayer house in Oleśnica, but the nearest cemetery was in Stopnica. They didn't have far to go – about six kilometres. Jews had been living in Stopnica since the sixteenth century. As much as 75 per cent of the population was Jewish. In September 1939 approximately 2,600 Jews lived there. In 1940 the Germans executed 13 Jews at Passover. The Jewish population there rose to 3,200 as a result of deportations. In November 1942, 400 Jews were executed and 1,500 sent to labour camps. Those who remained were deported to Sandomierz in 1943.

At the same time, the Jews were transported out of Oleśnica. More of them lived in the town than before the war, since the Germans had resettled several families from nearby villages. That was how Józef Mandelman's family, who had lived in the village of Strzelce, came to be in Oleśnica. Józef had a lumber mill and a farm in Strzelce. When the Jews were resettled, some people realized what lay in store for them and fled to the forests. That was what the Goldsztajn brothers did, and so did Gdałka. Before the deportation to the death camps, a German named Andrzej Rezler drove into Oleśnica at dawn one morning. He robbed the Kac family and then took them to the nearby woods, where he murdered them. Despair engulfed the Jews. They could feel the circle of death closing in around them.

Then came the day of deportation. All the Jews had to assemble on the main square in Oleśnica. The Germans loaded them on to horse-drawn carts. Rzepecki's apartment had a window overlooking the square. 'We stood horrified behind the curtains, watching what they were doing to the Jews,' Rzepecki says. 'We saw Józef Mandelman's mother and his brother Jakub getting on to one of the carts. They glanced up at our window. They knew that we were sheltering Józef. That is how I still remember them all: looking in despair at a closed window.'

Only at night did Bronisław Rzepecki have contact with the Mandelman family. It was usually Józef's brothers-in-law who came to see him. Józef's wife came on other occasions. Mostly, they came to get food. Rzepecki also sometimes acted as an intermediary when the Mandelmans needed some of the money that they had deposited with the parish priest in Oleśnica, Father Antoni Król. The Mandelmans changed their hiding place after several months at Rzepecki's. They moved to the village of Jarosławice on the other side of the Wschodnia River. They had to cross the bridge at Młynczyski during the night. On the way, they encountered resistance fighters from the peasant battalions. In Jarosławice, Józef Maślanko helped the Mandelmans. They stayed there until the end of the German occupation.

When the war broke out, Bronisław Rzepecki was working as the secretary of the local government office in Oleśnica. Once the Germans arrived, they summoned him to the office of the military commandant in Stopnica. Rzepecki remembers that day. A Jewish milkman whom everyone knew was being burned at the stake on the main square of the little town. The commandant ordered Rzepecki to 'establish order and calm'. Rzepecki also had a meeting with the new mayor of Stopnica, who turned out to be on the anti-German side. He allowed Rzepecki to take one of the radio receivers that had been confiscated. Rzepecki installed it in a heating stove in the school house. That was the beginning of resistance activity in Oleśnica. They listened to London initially, and relayed the news through a network of contacts. Several months later a partisan unit, known as the Jędruś band, went into operation in the vicinity. This unit was the nemesis of those who collaborated with the Germans. The partisans ambushed and killed Andrzej Rezler, who had murdered Poles and Jews, on the forest road from Rytwiany to Sielec.

Just before Christmas 1940, Władysław Cybiński of Busko came to visit Rzepecki. He brought a friend along. The stranger turned out to be commandant of the Busko region of the Home Army. He was a major who went by the *nom de guerre* 'Srogy', which means 'Harsh'. Rzepecki was sworn into the movement by the major. He was given the cover name 'Aleksander', and assigned to organize a local unit to fight against the occupier. He remained active until the end of the war. The Red Army arrived, accompanied by the NKVD, and that signalled the beginning of deportations to Russia of resistance fighters from the Polish Home Army and the National Armed Forces. One day, secret policemen from the Security Bureau in Rytwiany came to Rzepecki's apartment. Fortunately, he was not at home.

That was when Rzepecki tracked down Józef Mandelman, who was staying in Leżajsk with his family. Mandelman agreed to travel to Lublin to meet with Józef Maślanko, who had become a minister in the provisional government there. Maślanko heard him out, and then called in an NKVD officer and requested that Rzepecki's name be crossed off the list of people accused of having murdered Russian commandos and Jews. Mandelman told the Russian about how Rzepecki had saved his life. Rzepecki's name was removed from the list, and Maślanko wrote a letter to the Security Bureau in Busko, asking them to leave Rzepecki alone. He also wrote to the governor of Kielce province and recommended that a job be found for this good citizen of people's Poland.

After the Kielce pogrom, the Mandelmans emigrated to Italy. Rzepecki and his family moved to Poznań.

Józef Mandelman did not know that the Rzepeckis had moved. He finally located them and wrote, in his first letter, on 25 December 1949: 'I have been looking for you and could not learn anything. I wrote several letters to many of our common acquaintances, but without any results. I was tormented by the thought that my friends would accuse me of failing to remember the kindness shown to me amidst misfortune. My dear Bronisław, I feel well here in the full sense of the word. Sometimes, however, I miss all of you with my mind and my heart both.'

Bronisław Rzepecki was invited to the Dutch embassy in 1984 to receive the Righteous Among the Nations of the World medal.

4 Krystyna's Heart

Adela: 'I was born in Radom on 10 April 1924. My name was Adela Pesa Reich. My father was Fajwel and my mother was Rywka (her maiden name was Moszkowska). My brother Józef was born on 20 August 1922, and my younger sister, Hana, on 29 December 1926. In 1929 our whole family moved to Bydgoszcz, where we lived at 6 Toruńska Street. Before the war, I began attending secondary school at the Marie Curie–Skłodowska grammar school. My father was a merchant in the leather trade. We fled from Bydgoszcz on 3 September 1939. We stopped in Włocławek and Łódź before finally arriving in Warsaw.'

Emilia: 'Because of my father's job, we lived in different towns. But my mother always travelled to Poznań to give birth to her children. We were all born at our grandmother's. To this day, we say, "That was our family maternity ward." I was born in Poznań and so were my two sisters, Krystyna, who is older, and Kazimiera, who is younger than me. We lived in Bydgoszcz before the war broke out. My father was director of the bus station there. My sister Krystyna began attending the Marie Curie–Skłodowska grammar school. Adela Reich was her best friend. When the war broke out, we fled to Warsaw. My father found an apartment at 15 Odolańska Street, in the Mokotów district.

In Warsaw, the Nogaj family joined the resistance movement. The parents were members of the Home Army, and the daughters belonged to the Grey Ranks scout movement. They kept weapons and clandestine publications in their apartment and in the basement. There were secret classes and training sessions. The girls were preparing to act as couriers and nurses.

When Adela came to see them the first time, Maria Nogaj told her: 'This is your home, too. You will always find shelter here.' So it was throughout the occupation, until the deportation of the civilian population after the failure of the 1944 Warsaw Uprising.

In 1991 Emilia and Kazimiera learned that Adela had nominated their mother, Maria Nogaj (who lived in Poznań) and their sister Krystyna for the Righteous Among the Nations of the World medal. They felt embarrassed. 'This is because we were used to working in the resistance movement,' Emilia recalled. 'Sheltering Adela and helping her family was nothing unusual for us. We were always helping somebody, whether that meant finding food for them or obtaining false identity papers. That was our daily work. We were certainly not the sort of people who performed heroic deeds during the occupation.'

Adela: 'Fischer signed the decree about the establishment of a Jewish district on 2 October. We had to live there. We were given several days to move. The district was sealed off from the rest of the city on 16 October, and armed guards were placed at the gates. A 3-metre-high wall topped with barbed wire was built around the ghetto. My parents and brother and sister lived in the Jewish district. Having the "best looks" of the family, I remained on the Aryan side in order to get food for the others. On the day that they sealed off the ghetto, the Germans organized a police operation, commanded by Waldemar Schön, in search of Jews who were in hiding. On the first day, they confiscated over 4,000 Jewish shops and about 600 workshops on the Aryan side. Jews were being rounded up and that was why I obtained false documents under the name of "Halina Pilaczyńska" as quickly as possible.'

Adela Reich visited the Nogajs frequently. She obtained food for herself and for her family in the ghetto. Krystyna and

Emilia used odds and ends of wool to knit socks for Adela and her sister Hana. At the time, their father was a driver for the Central Fish Warehouse, which stood adjacent to the ghetto. Mr Nogaj frequently tossed food through the window to his acquaintance, the tailor from Bydgoszcz. On one occasion, Nogaj saw some people who were starving to death and asked, 'Why don't you share the food with them?' The tailor answered, 'I only give it to those who might survive.'

In the same building on Odolańska Street, there lived a homosexual, Stefan H. Emilia Nogaj cannot recall the circumstances under which Adela made the man's acquaintance and entrusted him with some of her valuables. When Adela wanted to get them back, Stefan H. refused. Adela told the Nogajs what had happened. Some time later, the man was found dead with a gunshot wound to the head. Emilia Nogaj does not believe that the underground executed him because of Adela. She recalls that he was seen frequently in the company of German officers. His death probably resulted from those contacts.

On the Aryan side, Adela lived under constant pressure. She feared being recognized or blackmailed, and having to change apartments yet again. She feared the men whose eyes were always searching for people of suspect appearance. It was always the same. Either they followed their victims to their apartments, or they dragged them into a stairwell to strike a bargain. The price of silence was always whatever the victims possessed at the moment. And Adela always needed money. It increased the chances that her family, behind the walls of the ghetto, might survive.

The first of the operations aimed at liquidating the Warsaw ghetto began in late July 1942. Adela managed to stay in touch with her family until 5 August. The following day, while she was on the Aryan side, her family were forced to go to Umschlagplatz, loaded into cattle-trucks and taken to Treblinka. Her father Fajwel, her mother Rywka, her brother Józef and her sister Hana. All of them.

That was the day when Janusz Korczak's orphanage was taken to the Umschlagplatz. In all, more than 10,000 people were deported, the Reich family among them. It was such a great mass of people that Adela never found out whether the Reichs even saw the orphans and the Old Doctor. What she does know is that it was suffocatingly hot on the day they travelled to Treblinka in that gigantic transport. How hot it was for her parents, Józef and Hana in the cattle-trucks she could only guess.

Adela: 'I applied to the Meinl firm, where all the employees were Polish. I was assigned to the food warehouse, where I worked from six in the morning until six in the evening. I was living with a single lady at 15 Mokotowska Street. We slept in the same room. After work, I would stop at Krystyna's. There, I helped them prepare parcels for prisoners of war. On 4 May 1944, I fled from Warsaw in great haste. I had been warned that the Gestapo knew about my family background and where I lived. I escaped to the village of Rytwiany, near Jędrzejów. My aunt, a Warsaw housewife, was there. I worked as a maid. I wrote to Krystyna in July and signed the letter 'Adela'. The letter was intercepted by a postal employee who was a spy for the Gestapo and particularly interested in me. He recognized me. I had to escape from Rytwiany back to Warsaw, arriving in the city at 11 o'clock in the morning, on 1 August. The Uprising began at four in the afternoon. I reported to a medical unit. I was a courier and orderly at the Knights of Malta Hospital. I was unaware of the fact that, at the same time, Krystyna was an orderly at the field hospital on Mokotowska Street. When that hospital was bombed, she transferred to the Knights of Malta. That was the first time we had run into each other during the Uprising. Afterwards, we never parted.'

After the defeat of the Uprising, the Germans loaded 2,800 of the most seriously wounded and ill hospital patients into cattle-trucks and sent them to the camp at Zeittheim. Adela and Krystyna went with them. The Poles were quartered among Russian prisoners of war suffering from tuberculosis and Italians with syphilis. On the first day after arrival, the

Germans checked all new arrivals to see if there were any Jews among them.

Emilia Noga had been a courier in the Uprising. She left Warsaw along with her mother and her sister Kazimiera in the civilian march towards Pruszków. 'At a certain moment,' Emilia remembers, 'I saw a woman coming out of a bakery with two loaves of bread. I ran up to her shouting, "Please sell me that bread, ma'am." When I returned to the column, the civilians around me tried to tear the bread out of my hands. A German policeman came to my defence, using the butt of his rifle. To this day, I cannot understand it. How could the civilian inhabitants of Warsaw want to steal bread from me, a young girl who had been fighting to make their city free?'

Now, Emilia wants to tell about her father. The unit in which he was fighting captured several German soldiers in the Mokotów district. They were short of food. Her father took the scraps that the partisans left on their plates, mixed them with water, and gave the food to the German prisoners. When he ended up in Pruszków after the fall of the Uprising, he ran into one of those former prisoners. The German recognized him and allowed him to join his family instead of being sent to a camp.

Emilia also wants to tell about Skawina. That is where she and her mother ended up. They stayed there until liberation. Emilia recalls the last days and hours of the occupation. The Germans were desperately trying to get away. That was when Emilia first saw Poles offering them food, and inviting them into their homes to warm themselves by the stove.

Krystyna and Adela were in the Zeittheim camp at the time. Eighty women were crowded into their barrack. One of them knew that Adela was Jewish. This was a woman who had been wounded in the 1944 Warsaw Uprising. One day, she began screaming so that the whole barrack could hear: 'You Jewess! My daughter died, and you're still alive. If you die, no one will grieve for you. I can't stand the sight of you.' Adela was terrified, because four Jews had already been turned over to the Germans in the camp. From that day on, Krystyna kept her eye on the woman, to make sure that she did not tell the Germans about Adela.

The carpet bombing of Dresden began on 12 March 1945. Bombers flew over the camp. It was eight in the evening. A sentry fired warning shots at their barrack. He wanted to warn them that their windows were not blacked out properly. A bullet ricocheted and struck Krystyna in the heart. Adela ran for a doctor, but it was too late. Adela was allowed to accompany Krystyna to the camp cemetery.

When she returned to the barrack, she looked at Krystyna's bunk. There was nothing there, not the smallest thing to remember her by. She begged the other women: 'At least give me her picture.' She returned to Poland empty-handed.

5 Black Sunflowers

The little girl was found in an empty freight car at the train station in Milanówek. A Polish Red Cross courier gave the Jewish child to the Kaczmarek family, who lived in the Wielkopolska region. After the war, they moved back to Sieraków. In 1948 a representative of the Central Jewish Committee came for the child, and two years later, the little girl left for Israel.

Franciszek Kaczmarek was a master chimney sweep and his wife Stanisława was a homemaker. They raised five children. Franciszek volunteered for things. He founded the Volunteer Fire Company in Sieraków. He was secretary of the Sodality of St Anne and a member of the board of the Cooperative Savings Bank. When the war broke out he received a conscription notice. He came home after the Polish defeat in September 1939. Initially, the German police kept him at their precinct house. Like many other people from Sieraków, he was being held hostage. Had there been any acts of sabotage, Franciszek would have been shot.

On 12 December 1939, the Kaczmareks heard a pounding at their door. Local *Volksdeutsche* burst into their apartment and stood Franciszek up against the wall. They beat him, demanding that he turn over his weapons. Then the German sympathizers gave the family a few minutes to pack. The Kaczmareks left with only the clothes on their backs. On the way out, someone took the down-filled bedclothes. The Kaczmareks were taken to the market square and then carried by horse-drawn cart to the station in Międzychód. They got off the train in Szymanów, near Niepokolanów and spent Christmas at the monastery there. That was when they met Father Maximilian

Kolbe,[1] who was looking after another group of refugees from Sieraków. In January, they were resettled in nearby towns. The Kacmareks were taken to Żyrardów, where they stayed until the end of the war. When the Kaczmareks arrived there, the Germans had already resettled about a thousand Jewish people from other Polish towns in Żyrardów, where some 3,000 Jews had lived at the outbreak of the war. In February 1941 they were all taken to the Warsaw ghetto.

The Kaczmareks belonged to the Home Army. They risked their lives in the resistance movement. Stanisława Kaczmarek therefore decided: 'If my children survive the war, we will take in and raise one orphan.'

Transports of people passed through Żyrardów. They were on their way to forced labour or the gas chambers. The Kaczmarek children were assigned to give these people food and drink. Their daughter Janina recalls: 'We sneaked up close to a train one day. A window opened and a mother gave us her infant child. The woman knew that the train was on its way to a death camp. She wanted to save her child. I was holding the baby in my arms when the train began to move. That was when the woman started screaming that she wanted her child back. Someone took it from my arms, ran to the train, and gave it back to its mother.' Janina returned in tears to her own mother and told her what had happened. A Polish Red Cross Courier from Milanówek was listening to their conversation. This woman already knew about Stanisława Kaczmarek's resolution, and told her that the Red Cross frequently received war orphans. They decided to remain in touch. But no one thought that things would happen so quickly.

The child was found in an empty train carriage at Milanówek station. The carriage had been uncoupled from a train full of people on the way to a camp. No one remembers the details after all these years. One thing is certain: a small, black-haired girl was sitting in the empty train. The woman serving as a Polish Red Cross courier took her under her protection, and sent word to the Kaczmareks: 'There is a child for you.'

Stanisława went by buggy to pick up the child. When she walked into the room, she heard the courier saying, 'Basia, your mama's here.' The little girl was pale and emaciated, and had lice. 'The wide eyes of a frightened animal peered out from under her curly hair,' Janina remembers. The child was afraid of everyone and everything. She did not want to get into bed the first night. She fell asleep curled up on the floor. She woke up during the night, screaming in terror. Stasnisława took her into her own bed, pulling the covers over her and holding her tight, the way a mother does.

For the first two days the little girl would not speak. At last, she uttered a sentence that everyone in the Kaczmarek family knows by heart: 'Basia hasn't eaten, and Basia hasn't drunk anything.' She repeated those words for several weeks, even when she was not hungry.

In the beginning they could communicate with Basia only in German. She told them that she lived on Jagiellońska Street in the Warsaw ghetto. Her surname was Rephund, Rephud, or Rebhud – she spoke indistinctly. But she told them how German police had come into their apartment. They had beaten her father, and later put him in a 'box' – a coffin? Her mother's legs had been 'cut off' or 'docked', like a horse's tail. A 'white auntie' had taken her and put her on a train. The story was very muddled. What did she mean when she said that her mother's legs had been 'docked'? Who was the 'white auntie'? How had she come to be on the train?

Days, weeks and months passed. The little girl grew the way she should. Many of the neighbours knew that she was Jewish, yet no one informed. The Kaczmareks lived across the street from the German barracks. Perhaps this is why there were almost never searches or round-ups in the vicinity. They were fortunate enough to see the end of the war together and to return to Sieraków with Basia. When she reached home, Stanisława Kaczmarek believed that the little girl would always stay with them, but this was not to be.

When the time came for the little girl to start school, the Kaczmareks decided to adopt her. The parish priest in Sieraków advised them that they should first put an announcement in the newspaper, in search of Basia's parents. They took his advice. No one from Basia's family replied to

51

the advertisement. Instead, a representative of the Central Jewish Committee arrived. He told the Kaczmareks that the Jews appreciated what they had done for the little girl, but that the child should now return to her own people. A married couple from Łódź, who had lost their own child during the war, declared a willingness to take her. First, however, she was placed in the Jewish Orphanage in Otwock. The Himmels took her from there in September and adopted her.

Stanisława Kaczmarek could not accept what had happened. Her daughter Janina says years later: 'It was human evil that convinced her. The children in Sieraków made fun of Basia, shoving her, pulling her hair, calling her "Jewess".' Stanisława Kaczmarek thought that she might indeed be better off among her own people. At first, she made several trips to Łódź, to help Basia adapt to her new parents. But the heartbreak was too much for her to bear.

In 1950 she got a letter from Łódź. Basia's new parents, the Himmels, wrote 'We are going to Israel.' Stanisława wrote back immediately: she wanted to say goodbye. But the letter came back with the annotation: 'Addressee moved abroad.'

No one wrote to them from Israel. It seemed that they had lost contact with Basia forever. Remigiusz Pawelczak wrote an article in the monthly magazine *Pojezierze* about how the Kaczmareks had saved a Jewish child. He noted with some bitterness: 'Basia has probably lived in Israel for 40 years. She has surely forgotten many of the details of her life. She probably has children of her own. Like every true mother, she loves them and takes comfort in them. Basia certainly does not put up a Christmas tree. But the thought of the Christmas tree must frequently call to mind her Polish mother, her Polish father and her Polish brothers and sisters.'

'Nowadays, I remember her every Christmas Eve. There is never a holiday when we don't talk about Basia in our family,' says Janina Kaczmarek-Michalska.

Basia's name is Pnina Gutman, and she lives near Tel Aviv. She has two daughters. She began searching for her biological parents after the Himmels died. In a coffee shop on Allenby Street in Tel Aviv, she shows me pictures from Sieraków and says, 'I remember only two years of my Polish childhood, after I was adopted. The earlier memories are only isolated images: a Polish family, church, the orphanage in Otwock, a young boy who came on vacation in a sailor's suit and had an anchor tattooed on his arm. Now I know a great deal more about myself. In three months of searching, I have found four years of my life. But I still do not know what I did during the first two and a half years of my life.'

When Pnina was beginning the search for her parents, Lea Balint was organizing the Children Without Identities organization in Jerusalem, under the auspices of the Museum of the Ghetto Fighters' Kibbutz. Lea left Poland in 1950, when she was twelve. During the war she was rescued by Polish nuns, who hid her in their convent.

Lea tells me about how she produced a programme entitled 'Children Without Identities' for Israeli television. She shows me lists of children who were sheltered in convents and taken from there by Polish families. 'Do we have the right to reveal their identities?' Lea asks. 'Is it our duty as Jews to take the moral obligation upon ourselves and reveal the Jewish backgrounds of people who have maintained their Christian identity for 50 years, unaware of their personal tragedy? Are we under an obligation to explain the history of his or her background to every person who was rescued and is living in a Polish family, so that these people can have the right to choose?'

It was almost midnight. I could hear strange sounds outside the window. It sounded like the baying of dogs, or the howling of jackals. 'Come out on to the balcony,' Lea said. 'Look down there. Towards Yad Vashem. The Bratzlav Hasidim meet in that valley. They always come at night. They come to shout at God. They are in despair because their rabbi is gone.' That was when I recalled Zbigniew Herbert's poem about the little town of Bratzlav among the black sunflowers. 'I am seeking you, rabbi,' I repeated after the poet. The Hasidim in that poem reply: 'He is not here, he died a beautiful death, as if he were running from one corner to the other corner, all black, with the flaming Torah in his hand.'

That was when Lea told me about Pnina Gutman. About Pnina, who has no parents. 'She phoned on Holocaust Day,' Lea says. 'She told me about herself, about her foster parents and the fragments of memory. She told me how she found her papers in the Jewish Historical Institute in Warsaw. She already knew that she had been looked after by the Kaczmarek family from Sieraków, and that her name had been Basia Kaczmarek.'

Pnina had to travel to Poland. It was a warm June day. She hired a car. When she arrived in Sieraków, she sent the driver to find the Kaczmareks' son. When she saw the 70-year-old man standing before her, with an anchor tattooed on his arm, Pnina Gutman cried out: 'Bogdan!'

NOTE

1. Father Kolbe (1894–1941) was the founder of the Catholic publishing centre in Niepokolanow, and a former missionary to Japan. He was interred in Auschwitz, where he died. Kolbe was beatified in 1971 and canonized in 1982.

PART II
Rings of Memory

6 What Happened on Chłodna Street?

It is 21 July 1942 in Warsaw. A Tuesday – the day before the first liquidation operation in the ghetto. Doctor Polak calls on Professor Franciszek Raszeja to ask for help in diagnosing a patient in the ghetto. He has a pass issued by the German police. (He paid no attention to the policeman who warned him: 'Don't go into the ghetto. It's going to be hell in there.)

In the meantime, a cordon of police surrounds the Jewish district, and only six of the 22 checkpoints remain open. At ten o'clock on the morning on 22 July officials of the Einsatz Reinhard staff from Lublin, under the command of Herman Hoefle, appear in Czerniakow's office in the Jewish community building. They notify Czerniakow of the deportations, and demand that thousands of Jews be assembled at the Umschlagplatz. (Adam Czerniakow takes his own life the next day.) The operation begins and lasts until September. The number of victims is estimated at 275,000. Of this figure, 254,000 Jews are murdered in Treblinka. There are 200 known cases of suicide.

The patient in the ghetto is Abe Gutnajer, a well-known Warsaw antique dealer. He lives on Chłodna Street. Raszeja and Doctor Polak leave for the ghetto in the afternoon. They probably enter through the checkpoint on Żelazna Street, or perhaps at Grzybowska. They reach Chłodna Street without encountering any difficulties. The street is still a transit route for the Aryan part of the city, but a high wall separates the pavement from the street itself. The two sides of the street, and the two parts of the ghetto, are connected by a wooden bridge. The bridge is as high as the third floors of the buildings (as Mary Berg notes in her New York journal). If Abe Gutnajer lived at no. 6 Chłodna Street, then Raszeja and Doctor Polak would have had to cross the bridge.

Around Abe Gutnajer's bed stand Professor Raszeja, Doctor Polak, a nurse and the patient's family. A consultation is in progress. Then at about 7 o'clock, Gestapo agents from Lublin burst into the apartment. According to one version, Raszeja reaches into his pocket for his pass when he sees the Germans. The Germans misinterpret his action and kill everyone in the room. There is another version, provided by the underground periodical *Sprawa* (The Cause): Latvian auxiliaries and SS troops surround the building. The tenants are driven out of their apartments into the courtyard. They have all been sentenced to death. The reason given is that the occupants of the building are engaged in food-smuggling. Both physicians protest and show their identity papers, but they are nevertheless shot and killed, along with the gravely ill patient and his family.

At Fischer's trial after the war, witness Maślanko explained: 'The Germans were searching for prominent Jews on Chłodna Street that day. Some were arrested and taken to Pawiak prison. Some were shot outside their buildings.' Maślanko was not certain whether or not Raszeja was shot in the apartment. He also gave a different address: 26 Chłodna Street.

There is also a letter extant from T. Bednarczyk. He writes that the Gestapo was looking for wealthy people to rob. That is what led them to Gutnajer's apartment. Furious at finding inconvenient witnesses there, they shot everyone. Another source provides the following interpretation of events: 'Professor Raszeja was well known in Germany. It is hard to believe that his death was purely accidental, all the more so because the German authorities knew that he was then in the ghetto.'

In his *Chronicle of the Warsaw Ghetto*, Ringelblum notes that in March 1941: 'The well-known owner of one of the largest Hebrew book collections died.' The notes indicate that this is a reference to Abe Gutnajer. However, the dates do not agree. Ringelblum notes that he died heart-broken about the books he left behind on the Aryan side. In fact, we do not know what illness Gutnajer was suffering from. Perhaps it was tuberculosis, or it could have been heartbreak. It would have been a beautiful thing to die in the ghetto of heartbreak over one's books. Ryszard Löw of Tel Aviv, who writes in such a lovely way about the Jewish booksellers and their cult of the book, would have said: 'What's so strange about that?'

Bożena Raszeja-Wanic is the professor's eldest daughter. She was twelve in 1942. She remembers that July evening, and the way her mother was afraid. At home, they knew that their father had gone into the ghetto. The hours passed. It got late. Her mother was increasingly impatient. She phoned the Red Cross Hospital on Smolna Street, where Raszeja worked. No one knew anything. Finally, Doctor Dąbrowska came to see them on Rozbrat Street. She mentioned some sort of rumours from the ghetto. The next day, Mrs Raszeja went to collect her husband's body. The professor was buried at Powązki Cemetery. 'Half of Warsaw came out to pay its respects,' Doctor Bożena Raszeja says, 'he was the poor people's doctor. He founded the Bone and Joint Tuberculosis Clinic for them.'

Franciszek Raszeja was educated at the classical *gymnazjum* in Chełmno. Later he studied at the universities of Berlin, Munster, Cracow and Poznań. At the latter institution, he earned his diploma as doctor of all medical sciences in September 1923. Three years later, he married Stanisława Deniszczuk, and 13 years later he became professor of orthopaedics. In 1937 he joined ten other Poznań scholars in signing a protest letter against 'the principle of the ghetto bench'. He was the sort of person who had the courage of his convictions.' This was not easy in Poznań, which was dominated by the National Democrats who constantly warned the populace about the 'Jewish red' steamroller threatening them from the east.

The Raszeja family came to Warsaw from Kowel. Earlier, in the first days of the war, the professor had been mobilized as a military physician and ordered to Łódź. Together with his field hospital, he had been evacuated from there to a small town in Volhynia. Bożena Raszeja remembers how the trip to Kowel, in cattle-trucks, took two weeks. Her father was appointed commander of the hospital.

In those years, half the residents of Kowel were Jews. The Raszejas were quartered with a Jewish family. In November a Jewish acquaintance warned her parents: 'Get out of Kowel, because the Russians will be here soon. The hospital will be liquidated and the officers imprisoned.' Bożena recalls how they crossed the River Bug at night in a boat. Then they rode a cart to Warsaw. At first, they stayed with her mother's family. Her father reported for work to the Ujazdowski Military Hospital. In December he became chief physician in the surgical ward at the Red Cross Hopsital at 6 Smolna Street. He set up a 30-bed orthopaedic ward where students attending a clandestine medical school were trained. He also cooperated with Ludwik Hirszfeld in running a secret blood-donation station for Jews living in the ghetto. The Raszejas moved soon afterwards to 9 Rozbrat Street, but were evicted from that apartment the day after Franciszek was murdered.

Stanisława Raszeja brought her daughters Bożena and Ewa back to Poznań in February 1945. They went to their home in the Wierzbięcic district, but there was nothing left except rubble.

Just when it seemed to Franciszek Raszeja's daughters that they knew everything there was to know about their father's death, they came across an account by Doctor Zbigniew Lewicki. During the occupation, Lewicki worked at the Red Cross Hospital in Warsaw. In the 1970s he came from his home in the suburbs of Montreal to visit Doctor Stefan Wesołowski. Three hours before the liner *Stefan Batory* was due to sail, Lewicki agreed to describe how Professor Raszeja's body was found. 'At around eleven o'clock at night,' Lewicki said, 'I received a phone call from the commandant of the Red Cross Hospital, Colonel Zygmunt Gilewicz, informing me that Raszeja had not returned from the ghetto. I immediately phoned the headquarters of the Jewish Police in the ghetto. The officer on duty, an acquaintance of mine, would not give me any concrete information. However, he warned me that it would be dangerous to go looking for the professor that night.'

The next day, Lewicki obtained a pass to the ghetto. In an office near Nalewki Street, he was given the address where the consultation had been held. He went to Chłodna Street and found the building empty. However, he found the care-taker, who led him up to the third floor and showed him Abe Gutnauer's apartment. The caretaker's account indicated that everyone there had been killed.

Lewicki told Wesołowski how he searched for Professor Raszeja's body: 'I went to the Jewish cemetery, and the care-taker there showed me the graves where some people, who had been shot, had been placed the previous day. All the corpses were covered with lye, but we managed to pick out the professor's body. He was dressed, but without shoes or documents. In his pocket, we found several small slides ... There was no doubt that he had died as a result of two gun-shot wounds, one in the middle of his forehead and the sec-ond above his right eye. The professor was a tall man, and it seemed that he had been shot while seated. I did not see any exit wounds.'

Getting the corpse out was no easy matter. However, city sanitation authority workers were allowed to enter the ghetto. They helped Lewicki remove the body in a city garbage truck. At around five in the afternoon, Lewicki placed the professor's body in the small chapel of the Red Cross Hospital. The entire staff of the hospital gathered around the bier.

On 10 June 1990, the Raszeja family was invited to Chełmno. A memorial plaque honouring the Raszeja brothers was unveiled on the building at 14 Main Square. The Germans had murdered Maksymilian, a professor of moral theology, in October 1939, when he refused to tell them where a copy of the Gutenberg Bible had been hidden. Franciszek, murdered in the Warsaw ghetto, had fought in the German army in 1914, been captured by the Russians and sent to Tashkent and the Urals before escaping and returning home by way of Petrograd, Finland and Sweden. Leon, the mayor of Toruń, had died in an air raid during the first days of the war. Only the fourth brother, Alojzy, survived the war.

7 'Run Father, or Else they'll Kill you'

The bullet entered the left side of the body. Ernst von Rath fell bleeding to the floor. The policeman standing at the entrance to the German embassy in Paris was notified. He managed to stop the young man who was hurrying out of the building on the Rue de Lille. The man's name was Herschel Grynszpan.

On the night of 27 October 1938 the German police detained around 17,000 Jews who were Polish citizens, and terminated their right of residence in Germany. The detainees were taken to stations, from where special trains delivered them to the German–Polish border. The timetables were arranged in such a way that the deportees arrived at the border by 29 October. From the nearest German towns, the Jews were led on foot to the border crossings. People who were travelling avoided deportation. Only in Leipzig did a large group of Jews receive advance warning and manage to flee from their dwellings to the consulate grounds. Since it was a small building, many of them spent the first night under the open sky, and subsequent nights in tents.

The Jewish deportees crossed the border in several places. For instance, almost 8,000 Jews were delivered to the border town of Neu Bentschen (Zbąszyń). After a journey of many hours, they were made to walk seven kilometres to the 'open border'. There, they waited several hours in the cold and rain until the Polish authorities made up their minds to admit them to Zbąszyń. A police report states:

> I hereby report that at 20.30 hours on 28 October 1938, the German authorities deposited 654 persons on the border along the Zbąszyń–Rogatka road. On the Polish

side, they were detained by the police at a distance of one kilometre from the border … At 21.00 hours, information was obtained that a second group of approximately 300 persons had crossed the border near the railroad tracks and was marching in the direction of Zbąszyń train station … More new groups of expelled persons arrived at intervals of 30–60 minutes along the Chlastawa–Nądnia road and the Zbąszyń–Neu Bentschen railroad tracks. It was determined that the expellees are Polish citizens of Jewish nationality …

Throughout the day on 29 October, there were group expulsions … The largest group, up to 700 persons, was expelled at 9.30 hours. This group sat down near the Polish border, on the Jewish side, and refused to enter Polish territory. Since the forces of the police and the Border Patrol were insufficient, the German authorities brought up an army company which fixed bayonets and moved up to attack the seated persons, beating and trampling them. With their bayonets and rifle butts, the soldiers forced the expellees to cross into Polish territory …

Among the Jews deported from Hanover to Zbąszyń was the Grynszpan family: Sendel and Rywka, the parents of the 17-year-old assassin, Herschel, and his sister Esther and brother Markus. Like many of the other people forced across the border, the Grynszpans lost the bundles they were carrying. Polish soldiers recalled that after they had forced the Jews across, the Germans began unloading all the parcels and suitcases that had been left behind. There must have been a great many of them, since the SS spent many hours combing the forests.

Sendel Grynszpan left his home in Poland and moved to Germany in 1911, at the age of twenty-five. After several years, he and Rywka (née Silberberg), settled in Hanover and opened a grocery store at 36 Burgstrasse. That was where their six children were born. At the time of their expulsion from Hamburg only three children remained alive: their daughter Esther, born in 1916; their son Markus, born in 1919; and their son Herschel, born in 1921. Sendel never went to the trouble of exchanging his documents and applying to the German authorities for naturalization. This was not because he longed for his Polish home town of Dmenin. He simply did not believe that such a fate could lie in store for him. In her book about the trial of Eichmann, *Eichmann in Jerusalem: A Report on the Banality of Evil*, Hannah Arendt quotes the testimony of Sendel, who miraculously survived the occupation by escaping to Russia:

> At eight o'clock in the evening on Thursday, 27 October 1938, a policeman called on us and ordered us to report to the Ninth Commissariat. 'Let's go right now,' he added. 'Don't take anything except your passports.' … They held us there until Friday evening … Next, they loaded us into police vans, into Black Marias, and took us to the train station. The streets were lined with people shouting '*Juden raus* – to Palestine!' We reached the border at six o'clock in the morning on the Sabbath day. … SS men were striking us with bullwhips and beating up anyone who lagged behind. The road was wet with blood. They pulled our suitcases out of our hands and treated us with unspeakable brutality. It was the first time I had seen such animal savagery among Germans. They shouted at us: 'Run! Run!' I was struck, and I fell into the ditch. My son helped me to my feet and said, 'Run father, or else they'll kill you.'

Zbigniew Mintzer, a journalist from *Tygodnik Ludowy* (The People's Weekly), described the forced exodus to the town of Zbąszyń:

> In the course of one night, the population of the city increased by one hundred per cent. Red Cross ambulances cruised the streets. Field kitchens could be seen. It looked like a town on the front lines. We went into a small brick building. Before the war, it was a stable for the military riding school. Now, several hundred people were living there. There were rows of straw mattresses along the walls. But there were far more people than

mattresses. The penetrating cold of the walls reached me through my warm overcoat. There was not a single heating stove in the large, high-ceilinged building. We stood in the middle, as if we were embarrassed by our fortuitous, unnecessary presence. A crowd of people with pale faces and feverish eyes slowly assembled around us. At first there was silence, and then an outburst of complaints, regrets and maledictions. Tears mixed with curses.

Jewish people walked around the small town in the clothes they had been wearing on the day when they were dragged from their homes in Hamburg, Cologne, Vienna, Berlin, and Hanover. They had been given only 20 minutes to pack, so they needed urgent help. The report submitted by Director Olasik of the Border Commission indicates that 1,500 people were quartered in the old barracks, 1,500 in Grzybowski's mill, 400 in the old school on Freedom Square, 100 in the prayer house, 120 in the sports hall and 250 in the indoor firing range. Local residents took in 700 Jewish lodgers, charging them 50 groszy per bed. On 30 October, 54 Jews were sent to the Rohr Jewish Hospital in Poznań. The supply problems were so severe that hay had to be ordered from distant estates.

On 31 October Jews were forbidden to depart from Zbąszyń, and the police set up checkpoints at the train station and along the roads out of town. A refugee aid committee, headed by Izaak Gitermann of Warsaw, had been in operation since the first days of the crisis. Its members included Emanuel Ringelblum, the future chronicler of the Warsaw ghetto.

The municipal memorial book, which is kept in the Zbąszyń museum, contains accounts by the expellees. One of them wrote: 'It was the night of 29–30 October. On that day, all the Jews who were Polish citizens were arrested. Without regard for their age, family situation, or state of health. They were allowed to take ten marks each.'

Ignacy Andrzejewski was on duty that day. He recalls how the Poles, too, felt helpless. 'The Jews had the German police, with bayonets fixed, behind their backs, and the [Polish] Border Security Corps, which initially did not want to admit them to their own country, in front of them. Only after the *starosta* (prefect) of Nowy Tomyśl intervened at the Foreign Affairs Ministry was the border opened to the Jewish expellees.

'The first days were very difficult,' recalls Franciszek Zierke, curator of the Zbąszyń Museum. 'Thanks to help from the local residents and the Jewish committee, however, all the expellees had roofs over their heads, food from the field kitchens, and medical services at the outpatient clinic. Some of the people left quickly to stay with relatives in central Poland. The normalization was attested to by the fact that a Jewish sports club, the Maccabees, was set up. The local Obra team played a soccer match against them and lost, 3–1. However, there were also cases in which the tragic predicament of the Jews was exploited. For instance, the owner of the bus that ran from the train station to the centre of town charged locals 50 groszy, but initially took two złoty from the Jews. There were other minor frictions, but there was never any sort of wide-scale action against the Jews.'

Jadwiga Kozłowska recalls how Zbąszyń became a little town that newspapers all over the world were writing about. Her father made a business trip to central Poland. When he told some Jews that he was from Zbąszyń, they opened their arms to him. 'We'll help you, because you helped our people.'

The first local newspaper to write about the Zbąszyń interest was *Kurier Poznański* (The Poznań Courier). Its correspondent wrote: 'The people are counting on the state authorities to prevent the importation within the borders of the Republic of more than ten thousand Jews.' The National Democrat press returned frequently to this unfriendly tone. *Gazeta Polska* (The Polish Gazette) proclaimed in its editorial:

We are facing the phenomenon of the influx to Poland of an element that, in the majority, is not associated with the Polish state either by birth, family, tradition, language or culture. The only tie that these people have to Poland is the possession of a Polish passport, which in many cases is invalid. We are thus facing the immigration to Poland of an alien element that, furthermore, is lacking in all means of existence.

Let us return to the *Poznań Courier*, the leading newspaper of the National Democrats. Several weeks after the incident on the border, the *Courier* reported that 'the Jews in Zbąszyń have nothing to do. They wander the streets all day jabbering loudly in their jargon or in German. They are depraving the local population which, because of economic poverty, can offer little resistance to Jewish money.' The correspondent concluded that 'there is a range of important reasons to liquidate in short order this mass Jewish concentration that has come into being in the land of Great Poland'.

The pro-government press confined itself for the most part to official communiqués, while opposition newspapers showed an interest in the plight of the exiles. The Jewish press, in turn, expressed appreciation for the attitude of the residents of Zbąszyń. H. Szoszkies wrote in *Nasz Przegląd* (Our Review): 'Polish railroad men cried, and Polish border guards wiped tears from their eyes when fainting mothers with babes in their arms, like hunted animals, embraced them. What a consolation it was to me to hear that ordinary people, Polish workers and peasants, showed so much sympathy to the tormented victims from the other side of the border.'

A National Committee for Aid to Jewish Refugees was formed. Communities and organizations were mobilized, in contrast to provincial government offices, which took little interest in the fate of the refugees. It was difficult, on the other hand, to expect much help from the Jews of Zbąszyń and the *powiat* (district) of Nowy Tomyśl, since the whole Jewish community of Nowy Tomyśl, Wolsztyń and Międzychód numbered barely 160 people. Many refugees reached Poznań, especially on the first day. The community and Rabbi Sender took them under their protection. The refugees most commonly found lodging and food in private apartments. Fira Sochaczewska, who lived on Kozia Street, recalls that her parents took in two Jews whose family lived in England. Noach Lasman was moved by the plight of the refugees to join the Hashomer Hatzair Zionist organization. He recalls that Jewish students taking part in the aid campaign were excused from classes at his secondary school. One such student was Henryk Kronenberg, who travelled with other members of the organization to deliver food, blankets and household utensils. Kronenberg also recalls that Poles helped, and mentions Jerzy Andrzejewski, Maria Dąbrowska, Maria and Józef Czapski and Maria Kuncewiczowa.

There were, however, other opinions, like that of Karol Zbyszewski, who wrote in the nationalistic *Prosto z mostu* (Straight Talk): 'This Nazi repression is necessary … Humanitarianism, gentleness, and liberalism are all well and good. But clearing the country of Jews is even better. This will never be accomplished without pressure, coercion, and decrees. If you do not want to be eaten by the bedbug, then you must crush it.' Jews from Poznań remember particularly well an article in which 'J.W.' wrote in a 'vile' way about the Jewish committee that was aiding the refugees:

This committee behaves in a disgusting way … It announces that it has exhausted its funds … The burden of maintaining the Jews from Zbąszyń is shifted to the Polish government, shifted to the citizens of Zbąszyń … The people of Zbąszyń have been caught in the lasso of mercy, and now that they are caught, the Jews are tightening the noose. At first, the committee paid one złoty for a night's lodging, and then it went down to 75 groszy, and then to 50, and then 30, and they say that they will soon pay nothing.

The article ends with invective that is hard to forget: 'Through the Zbąszyń trough, the Zbąszyń gutter, the Zbąszyń sewer, a new wave of parasites is flowing into Poland. Continually, uninterruptedly.'

To this day, historians ask what the authorities hoped to accomplish by detaining several thousand people, most of them Polish citizens, in a border town. All the more so, because that detention was seen in a very bad light by the international community, which was unsparing in its criticism of the Polish government. Nevertheless, the camp was liquidated very late – in August 1939. That was when the Grynszpans left Zbąszyń.

The Poznań historian Ireneusz Kowalski poses further questions. He is unable to detect any logic behind the way that permission was granted for refugees to leave Zbąszyń. In some cases, the *starosta* refused to grant permission to leave the camp to people who were ill, or who had spouses whom they could join. So it was with Sura Kosiorowska, who wrote in her petition: 'My husband lives in Łódź. It is very difficult for me to live here by myself, and my state of health is worsening by the day.' Nor did the *starosta* agree to Saul Rosenbaum's petition that a 6-year-old child be released to join its mother in Rzeszów.

Let us return to the Grynszpan family. On 31 October, Esther wrote a postcard that she sent on 1 November from Zbąszyń to her brother Herschel in Paris. Esther described her tragic predicament. The postcard reached Herschel on 3 November. The contents of that card are regarded as having prompted the 17-year-old Herschel Grynszpan to commit his dramatic deed. He stated as much in his testimony to the police: 'When I read that card, I realized what danger my parents were in. That was when I decided on an act of revenge and protest against a representative of the Reich.'

On 6 November Herschel moved out of his Uncle Abraham's home and rented a room in the Hotel Suez under the assumed name 'Heinrich Halter'. At 8.35 the following morning, he purchased a revolver at the A là Fine Lame (Good Edge) steel-goods shop. At 9.30 he asked an embassy official to arrange a meeting with one of the secretaries. Three minutes later, he walked into Ernest von Rath's office. When Rath asked what he wanted, Herschel replied, 'You are a filthy German, and I am now going to present you with a document on behalf of 12,000 persecuted Jews. He pulled the revolver from an inside pocket of his sports coat and fired five shots, aiming at the centre of von Rath's body. It was 9.45 in the morning. Von Rath was rushed to a clinic, where he died soon after. The police arrested Grynszpan. Goebbels' propaganda machine inflated the assassination to incredible proportions, as a preparation for Kristallnacht.

Grynszpan's motives were never fully explained. Many people supposed that his act was one of vengeance for the expulsion of 15,000 Jews, including his own family. 'But this is an unlikely explanation,' says Hannah Arendt, while reminding her readers that Grynszpan was a psychopath who, unable to finish school, was wandering around Paris and Brussels. There was also talk of a homosexual connection with the victim, but this could be wishful thinking on the part of the police. On the other hand, von Rath was a man of open anti-Nazi convictions. 'Perhaps,' Arendt says, 'Grynszpan became an unwitting tool of Gestapo agents in Paris who wanted to kill two birds with one stone – to create a pretext for a pogrom in Germany while simultaneously eliminating an opponent of the Nazi regime.'

The same day that Herschel shot von Rath, his sister Esther wrote another letter to him. (She had no idea of what had happened in Paris.) She wrote: 'We can't go on this way.' Since Esther's letter was addressed to her uncle, Abraham Grynszpan, with whom Herschel had been staying, Sendel himself added a note: 'We are miserable. We have fallen into poverty. We don't have enough to eat. You, too, have known poverty. Please, dear brother, think of us. I don't have the strength to bear this.'

8 Around the Circle

The telephone rang. 'I am a professor of sociology at the university in Toronto,' said the stranger, by way of introduction. 'I have come here with my father's sister to look for traces of our family in Poznań. We're staying in a hotel. Could you help us in our enquiries?' I made an appointment to meet Gottfried Paasche in the hotel lobby the next day.

Gottfried lived in Toronto. He came to Poznań with his aunt, Helga Paasche, who lived in Switzerland and was over 80. Gottfried was born in Japan and knew Poland mainly from family stories. For Helga it was different. She clearly recalled the family estate near Krzyż. To tell the truth, that area was not then a part of Poland. The story of her family, however, was linked closely to Wielkopolska. Motty[1] might well have been writing about her grandmother when he mentioned a female Jewish merchant named Witkowska, who was prominent in the silk trade. In the 1830s ladies thronged to her – and to Falk, Herman, and Königsberger – 'like Muslims to Mecca'. It was probably only ladies in a hurry who went to Witkowska's shop. The more self-respecting ladies, as Motty writes, 'ordered the goods brought to them'. In such cases, it was the shop assistant who entered the client's residence first, followed by the merchant with his great bundles. The material was laid out on the beds, tables and chairs, and the inspecting, fitting and bargaining began in earnest.

It is known for certain that Helga Paasche's great-grandparents were Ernestyna and Arnold Witkowski. Ernestyna was born is Skwierzyna, and her maiden name was Krakau. Arnold Witkowski, born in Poznań in 1815, was a Jewish merchant in the silk trade. He spent 38 years in Poznań, living there until 1853. We know very little about Arnold. Like many Jews, he moved from Poznań to Berlin, and we can therefore assume that he underwent the same process of assimilation as the majority of the Jews living in Poznań.

When Arnold Witkowski was entering adult life in the 1830s, Jews dominated commercial life in Poznań. They included such potentates as Wolf Eichborn (whose fortune was worth 10,000 thalers) and Solomon Auerbach (7,000 thalers), both of whom lived on Żydowska (Jewish) Street. Julius Munk, Mendel Schiff, Mendel Ephraim, Dawid Goldberg and Philippsohn were all merchants on the Old Town Square. Arnold Witkowski was eighteen when the law regulating the naturalization of Jews in the Duchy of Poznań came into force. One condition of naturalization was an obligation to use only the German language in all public affairs. When a Jew met this condition, he was defined as *judisch Deutsche*, or a 'Jewish German'. Naturalized Jews, the majority of whom were merchants, soon formed the new administration of the Jewish community in Poznań.

'Those were great years for Jewish merchants,' I explain to Gottfried Paasche. The wool market was opened in 1837. Michael Kantorowicz became the owner of the second largest bank in Poznań. Jewish merchants began to unite in the 1840s, and in 1843 they founded the Union/Institute of Jewish Commercial Service. Six years later, the word 'Jewish' was eliminated from the name of the organization – probably an indication that it had opened its membership to Christian Germans. The fortunes also grew. By 1860 most of the buildings around the Old Town Square belonged to Jewish merchants. The Kantorowiczes owned four buildings, the Goldbergs three, and the Ephraims two. By 1860, however, Ernestyna and Arnold Witkowski were already living in Berlin.

Helga and Gottfried Paasche were interested in the events of 1848, the 'Springtime of the Peoples'. Perhaps Helga's grandfather had had to choose between Germany and Poland then. The elderly lady from Switzerland will probably never find out. I remind her that it is impossible to state that the Jews of Poznań supported only the Germans during the Springtime of the Peoples. Things were more complicated than that. There were many friends and defenders of the Poles among the Jews. The physician Marcus Mosse supervised the defence of Grodzisk Wielkopolski, and Jews offered financial support to the Polish insurrectionist units forming in Miłosław. Yet there was more pro-German sentiment than pro-Polish. I tell Gottfried about the physician Robert Remak, who came from a poor Jewish family in Poznań. Motty writes that he 'not only was regarded as completely polonized, but also referred to himself as Polish, which was a great rarity then'. Motty left him in Berlin composing a resolution demanding that Polish prisoners in Moabit prison be freed.

Perhaps Arnold Witkowski was guided solely by economic considerations, we muse as we sit at a table in the Chimera Café. It is difficult today to recapture those times, and especially the motives of people who decided to leave Poznań for Berlin or other German cities. One thing we know for sure is that the Germans won the support of the Jews by promising them more and more rights. The fashionable Haskala (Enlightenment) ideas urging Jews to adopt the language and culture of the country they lived in were also significant.

When the Witkowskis had been in Berlin for three years, their son Richard was born. 'That's my grandfather', says Helga Paasche. The seventh of the Witkowski's children, Richard was born on 19 October 1856. The boy first attended Grutzmacher's private school, and then the *gymnazjum* from which he graduated in 1876. This is an important date. In the same year, he converted to Lutheranism and changed his name to Witting. Only later did his parents, sisters and most of his brothers take a similar step. His younger brother, Maximilian, a well-known journalist, adopted a different surname: Harden. Maximilian was the publisher of *Zukunft*, a leading weekly at the turn of the century. For his part, Richard Witting graduated from the University of Güttingen in law and administration. He married Gabriela Teuscher of Wittenberg. They had four daughters – Gabriela, Elen, Sybilla and Henrietta – and three sons – Richard, Axel and Klaus. One of the sons fell during the battle of Hollebek on 5

November 1914. Richard's career in administration began in Berlin, after which he was sent to Danzig for two years. In 1891 he was appointed mayor of Poznań. He held this office until 1902, when he returned to Berlin with the title of Privy Regency Councillor.

Historians are in no doubt as to Witting's services to the development of Poznań. On the other hand, the son of the silk merchant was one of the architects of local anti-Polish policy. Here is what the German historian Arthur Kronthal had to say about his contribution to the development of the city: 'He turned a backward, ugly little town into a neat, healthy city full of intellectual and artistic vigour, and pulsing with life and beauty.' It is said that Witting had regular office hours during which he received all citizens, regardless of their nationality, political views, or religion. His sense of fairness was appreciated not only by Germans but also by Poles and Jews. The affection in which he was held is attested to by his friendly relations with Archbishop Stablewski, whom many German historians regard as a Polish nationalist. In appreciation of his services, the citizens of Poznań awarded Witting the key to the city, and a street was named after him. A life-size portrait of Witting, painted by Professor Karl Ziegler, was hung in the city council chambers. In 1918 Witting Street was renamed Libelt Street, but the portrait of the mayor was left hanging in recognition of his services to the city. It was only taken down when the Nazis occupied the city in 1939. They may have been troubled by the Jewish origins of the mayor who died in 1923.

'He certainly felt at home in Poznań,' Helga Paasche says as she reflects on her grandfather Richard. 'After all, he was walking the same streets that his father, Arnold, had walked. His Jewish roots were here, by the Warta River. And his Polish and German roots as well. Perhaps that is why he gave Axel the middle name of Bogusław.'

'Now, let's talk about Gabriela, Richard Witting's eldest daughter. She was also my mother,' says Helga. 'She married Hans Paasche, a naval officer who was described by his friends as an "enthusiastic idealist". Hans knew what his countrymen were doing in Africa. From that time on, he became a critic of Prussian militarism. He had inherited land near the town of Krzyż from his father. Hans lived there during the war, and never made a secret of his pacifistic convictions. He maintained contacts with Polish workers and was accused of disloyalty to the German authorities. The fact that he was in a sanatorium when they came looking for him is what saved him. The war had just ended, and he was in Berlin working with the workers' councils. Four weeks after he left the sanatorium, his wife Gabriela died. He returned to Krzyż then and wrote his most profoundly anti-war articles. The whole time, he was on the blacklist of the German right wing,' Helga says. 'One day, the German police appeared at his estate of Waldfrieden to search for hidden weapons and communist literature. Hans was swimming in the lake. As he climbed naked from the water, the police shot him. It was supposedly an accident. There is no headstone on his grave anymore, because someone stole it. There is only a cross, with the inscription: "Here lies a man, a fighter for peace and understanding among people. Murdered for his convictions in 1920."' Helga was four years old at the time. When she was seventeen, she married a Swiss man. She changed her citizenship, which is what saved her life. Seventy-seven years after her father's death, she decided to visit Poznań. She wanted to learn the truth, for she knew that her family's documents were in the local archives.

Hans' wife Gabriela was the mother of four children. Jochan was born in 1911, Nies in 1913, Helga in 1916 and Iran in 1918. 'When Hitler came to power, Jochan was in law school,' Gottfried Paasche says of his father. '"That's the end of me," he thought, and switched to studying foreign languages. He learned Latin, Greek, Polish, Russian, Chinese, Japanese and Arabic.' He met Gottfried's mother, the daughter of a retired German naval commander, in 1934, on a Russian language course. 'My mother was studying agronomy, and was interested in Zionism. She even went to visit a kibbutz. But her father, who was half-Jewish, did not want to become involved in the Jewish–Arab conflict. When his mother was summoned by the Gestapo, they decided to leave Germany. They fled to Japan. I inherited my mother's Polish language textbooks.'

Sara is Gottfried's daughter. When she was nineteen, she 'discovered herself' through Judaism. She learned Hebrew, went to Israel, studied in a Jewish theological seminary and eventually became a rabbi. Sara's mother is a Jewish woman from New York. One of her forebears was named Baum and came from Poznań. 'That was like the closing of the circle,' says Gottfried Paasche, thinking about his wife, his Aunt Helga from Switzerland, the mayor of Poznań, and Mrs Witkowska, the mysterious silk merchant.

NOTE

1. Motty was an author of diaries describing life in ninetenth-century Poznań.

9 Blue Eyes

Maria Posiłek's father was a master craftsman in the Pinczewski brothers' factory. They say that he made dough. Dough was the mixture that was poured into the moulds. It was dried, taken out, and the doll was ready. It had only to be painted and dressed in pretty clothes. Marysia was then a small, inquisitive child. She would go to the factory so that she could peek through an open window and see what her father did there. One day, she ran into Mrs Pinczewska, who asked her, 'Do you know any rhymes?' Marysia paused a moment and recited a verse about the star of Bethlehem. The older lady was delighted. She said, 'You're going to grow up into a wise girl.' Then she called the master craftsman: 'Please give her a doll. The 75-centimetre one.' Marysia's father objected: 'But it's very expensive.' The older lady cut him off: 'Michał, it's a present!'

'Ah, what a wonderful doll that was! It had blue eyes, a little pink cap and white stockings. I ran home in ecstasy. The children surrounded me and a whole crowd of them escorted me. When my mother saw me, she nearly fainted. The doll was placed on top of the wardrobe. I burst out crying. I told my mother how I had recited a rhyme about the star of Bethlehem and little Jesus. My mother said: "But she's a Jew."

My father came home, and I listened in fear as he and my mother discussed the doll: "I'm sure they'll deduct it from your pay," my mother said. And my father replied, "Maybe they won't." And my mother: "They'll deduct it." And my father: "Maybe not." And my mother said: "If they deduct it, we'll give the doll back."

Saturday came. Payday. I ran to the factory. I waited a long time. Finally, my father came out, and I ran up to him. He smiled. "They didn't deduct it!" I screamed, and raced home.

I worried about the doll. I kept it from my brothers and sisters and hid it in the attic, along with my other treasures. During the fire on Starokaliska Street, the attic was destroyed, and that was the death of my doll. I would have gone into the fire after it if I had understood that I was going to lose it forever. But the doll has remained in my heart. When they told me at the university that factory owners were bloodsuckers, a voice inside me said: "No, that's impossible." I saw Mrs. Pinczewska before my eyes then. The good Mrs Pinczewska and her doll, which protected me from a belief in communism.'

Foolish Jędrek was a water-carrier who lived with us for a while. He was very thin, with dark eyes. He was always smiling. People used to shout after him: "Jędrek, Kasia had a Jew ..." To this day, I am not sure what those words meant. Perhaps it had something to do with his sister, who had a Jewish boyfriend. When the fire broke out in the houses along Starokaliska Street, my father carried Jędrek out of the flames after he was overcome with smoke inhalation. And afterwards he saved Jędrek's paralysed mother. My mother was urging him to save our possessions. "But there are people in there," my father said.'

'The war came. The Germans entered Opatówek, and Jews were forced to do hard labour on the town streets. One of the Pinczewski brothers was among them. When he bowed to me in greeting once, the sentry slapped him in the face. There came a day when they transported all the Jews to Koźminek. Our neighbours, the Szlamiaks, as well. Mother was very fond of them. She made up a food parcel and sent me to Koźminek. I knocked at their door. No one answered. I sat down on the doorstep. After a while, two little Jewish boys came along. I gave them the parcel. Some Jewish adults came running up. Perhaps they were the parents. They thanked me in such a special way that I can still see their faces.'

'Some 200–300 people worked in the Pinczewski factory, depending on economic conditions. That was where the women acquired good taste, by sewing costumes for the dolls.

They also learned about elegance. That was why, when you went out on to the street in Opatówek, you seldom saw a slovenly girl. The style was visible when the women strolled on the Long Market or walked to church along the Gillers' houses.

There were not many Jews in town. In 1921 only 186 residents were Jewish, out of a population of almost 3,000. Most of them died during the war. But there were some who managed to emigrate to Palestine in the 1930s. That's what Mrs Jarecka and her daughters did. Could it be possible that I saw one of them on television? It was many years ago, when they were showing victims of the war, or perhaps of some terrorist attack. She was standing there and lamenting over a dead child. But was it really Mrs Jarecka? Did fate hunt her down so far away?

Whenever I saved up a few groszy, I went to Mrs Jarecka's to buy paints. There were times when I heard them praying. How beautifully they prayed. I stood there hypnotized. I could hear the murmur of words from behind the door. I sometimes caught individual words: "*Adonai Elochemu, Baruch ata Adonai ...*". They prayed at home, because there was no prayer house in Opatówek. They gathered for communal prayers at the Szlamiaks'. Old Szlamiak was a splendid man. A beautiful Jew, with a long beard. And what wonderful beef he sold: pink, sliced in strips. A lovely pan-type scale stood on the counter. I remember how he stood there, bending over it with that enormous beard of his.

The Pinczewskis had a daughter named Łucja, and two sons, I think. They sent the girl to the University of Warsaw. I know that they managed to escape from the Nazis into the Soviet Union in 1939. Without the father, who died before the war. I never saw anyone from the Pinczewski family in Opatówek. Many years later, when I was house-cleaning, I found a portrait of Łucja Pinczewska's grandmother among papers set aside for burning.

I don't have any dolls from the factory. That's a shame, because they were lovely dolls. They had porcelain heads imported from Germany. They were very delicate, as if they were made from sea foam. Their cheeks were like rose petals. Mrs Nowakowska made beautiful wigs for them, but their eyes were made by Beksztajn, whom the Pinczewskis brought from Dresden. There were dark eyes, blue eyes, green eyes, and grey eyes. The biggest demand was for the blue. But those blue eyes weren't Jewish eyes. *Oy*, no they weren't.'

The last time that Maria Posiłek saw her dear friend Elżbieta Szlamiak was in Koźminek. Elżbieta wanted to give her a gold ring to remember her by. 'We'll never see each other again,' she said. 'I can't take it,' Marysia recoiled. 'After all, you got it from your Daddy for your tenth birthday.' The scene still haunts her. When she thinks about the war, the Pinczewskis, and Koźminek, she closes her eyes and sees dear, terrified little Elżbieta Szlamiak standing before her with the gold ring in the palm of her outstretched hand. Then Maria Posiłek asks herself: 'Where could I have hidden her?' There is silence. No one answers. 'Many years have passed since that day,' she says after a moment, 'and I am still looking for a hiding place for her.'

10 Threads of Memory

She has dug over 600 gravestones out of the ground. Some of them are in pieces. But since Łucja Nowak, curator of the Konin Museum, has had a computer she has managed to put some of the broken fragments of stone back together. She sometimes looks in wonder at the screen and finds that a piece of a gravestone bearing a name fits another piece with the dates of birth and death of someone who was previously unknown.

She has placed Jewish gravestones in Chełmno, in Konin Museum and in storage. (Some are lying on the grass in front of the museum.) There are gravestones from the cemeteries in Turek, Kleczew, Kłodawa, Dąbie, Dobra, Konin and Władysławów. Most of them, however, are still lying where the Germans placed them during the occupation. There are streets and pavements in Dobra, Dąbie and Kłodawa that are made out of gravestones. 'I don't have the money to recover them,' Łucja Nowak admits. When there are pavements made out of headstones, property-owners demand that new pavements be laid where the headstones are dug up. Sometimes the gravestones are rescued by friends of Łucja Nowak, such as the history teacher Radosław Głoszkowski of Kleczew. It was Głoszkowski who telephoned to say: 'Excavations have begun in a place where there are gravestones.' Nowak had earlier agreed with officials that they would notify her of work on the school playground. Things turned out the way she had supposed. The officials did not keep their word, but the teacher made it possible to save the gravestones.

Łucja Nowak sits in the archives and finds documents about the people she meets on the gravestones. She learns details: that Rojsa died of pneumonia; that someone's last sewing machine was confiscated because he failed to pay his taxes. The anonymous names blossom forth in human triviality.

She encountered Michał Fuks's family in the archives. Fuks was a rich Jew – there are certificates about his charitable donations. One of his sons was described in the 1821 census as a cloth and spice merchant. In 1835 he owned a house and capital worth 17,000 silver roubles. She found information about the first rabbi of Turku: a document related to an interrogation of him on 24 September 1836. She read that the rabbi of Dobra, Izaak Urbach, stopped in an inn. When local Jews began to assemble there, the mayor of Turku sent policemen there with a warrant for his arrest. The rabbi testified that he had only come to inspect the ritual slaughterer's knife. 'I have a wife, two children, and I live in Dobra,' Urbach said. The document indicates that he arrived in Turku at 10 o'clock in the morning of 22 September. He rented an apartment, using Juda Melken and Mojżesz Rozenfeld as his intermediaries. Although he had come only for a few days, he served as rabbi of Turku for 14 years. He was already acquainted with the inhabitants of the town, because their first cemetery had been in Dobra.

Marianna Poznańska, the daughter of Naftali Szotten, was born in Kalisz, in 1817. Her husband, Mosiek Poznański, was born in 1814, in Łódź, as was his father Gutman before him. Their wedding took place on 12 March 1837, when Maria was twenty. Łucja Nowak found the name of Maria's father, Naftali Szotten, mentioned in the interrogation of Rabbi Urbach, since he and Majer Gołąb signed pledges of security for the rabbi.

Majer Gołąb could not have been a rich man. Gołąb means 'pigeon', and in 1821 anyone who had any money could have chosen a better-sounding name. Those without money became Bułka (bun), Byk (bull), Dratwa (twine), or Fujar Mendel, 'ninny wheatsheaves' (a name that Łucja Mendel found in 1941 on a list of workers on a drainage project in Czachulec – the last reference to the man in question). Apart from Gołąb, there were Abram Jedwab (silk), Szmuel Kat (hangman), Leib Kołtun (mop-head), and Jakow Kibel (slop-bucket). Łucja Nowak has hundreds of Jewish names in her computer. All it takes is a movement of the cursor, and the names appear on the monitor: Malka Kochen, Jakow Kochen, and Efraim Kochen; Jakub Mordka Kompel; Dawid Landau (a merchant with 20,000 roubles capital in the 1835 census); Mojsze Lewiński; Abraham Menche; Izrael Mokotow (his beautiful gravestone lies in Chełmno); the Breslauer Rabbi (born in 1786, his first name was Rafael but his middle name is illegible); the Węgrów Rabbi (born in 1897, died in 1937; son of Cwi and Ariel).

Michał Berkowicz's family was noted in the 1821 census. Twenty years later, however, the members of that family were still having difficulty deciding on a permanent surname. The documents show that the Berkowiczes also went by the nickname 'Stempa'. In 1846, therefore, Michał Berkowicz had to reapply for the recognition of his and his sons' surname. Part of the family, however, stuck to the nickname, since 'Stempa' began appearing as a surname among the lists of residents.

On one of the gravestones that they recovered, Łucja Nowak and her assistants discovered the name of Ichoszi Glicenstein, – father of the sculptor, Henryk Henoch Glicenstein. That moment marked the beginning of her absorbing adventure in search of traces of the famous native of Turek. She asked for assistance from the Dreyfuss–Glicenstein Foundation in New York.

The earliest materials about the father of the sculptor were found in the little town of Dobra, several kilometres from Turek. The Glicensteins appear in the 1826 census as merchants and stall-holders. They were wealthy people with interests stretching from Gdańsk to Leipzig. They traded in grain, wood and wool. Their only problem was the lack of a male heir. In hopes of an heir, they made pilgrimages to holy places and gave generously to charity. Finally, the Most High heard their prayers. A son was born, and they gave him the names Ichoszi (Isaiah) and Alter. They gave the equivalent of the infant's weight in gold to the poor. Ichoszi grew into a devout man. He loved his six children and faithfully observed the rules by which they were raised. He helped the poor, often sacrificing the needs of his own family. Perhaps it is for this reason that the finances of the Glicensteins declined. Or perhaps this was due to the unworldliness of Isaiah, whose son Henryk wrote of him years later: 'He was renowned for his learning and piety. Despite the fact that he was impractical and incapable of coping with the everyday cares inherent in supporting his family, people came to him, even from afar, in search of his help and advice.'

Isaiah's wife Raja was a Berkowicz. Łucja Nowak found their name in a list of the Jewish families who lived in Turek. Raja was a beautiful and talented woman who had a strong influence on her son. She and her mother shared their youthful memories of the recovery of Polish independence. Little Henryk listened to stories of the approach of Napoleon's army and of the heroes of the January Insurrection. He and his friends played around a tree on the main square that was an object of reverence to the townspeople because it bore the bullet holes from when an insurgent had been murdered there on 21 December 1863.

Isaiah carved wooden toys for his children. His everyday job was at the quarry, where he made the gravestones that Łucja Nowak would discover in Konin. Henoch remembered the blocks of sandstone that lay in grandfather Berkowicz's garden, and wrote: 'I grew up and played among the stones that my father chiselled into gravestones. I carefully watched him as he worked. When I was ten years old, he put a hammer in my hand and I began to execute traditional ornaments like hands imparting a blessing, lions and candles. Wielding the hammer strengthened my delicate build.'

The carefree world of his childhood came crashing down in the course of a single night. A powerful hurricane swept through Turek destroying the synagogue in Dobra where he so loved to pray. His father Isaiah had to seek additional work to maintain his family. The 13-year-old boy left home and spent four years wandering from city to city. One stop on his route was Kalisz, where he stayed for a whole year. He supported himself by carving toys, chessmen and cane handles. In the end, he went to live with an uncle in Łódź, who was a teacher in a Talmudic school.

In 1994, Łucja Nowak delivered to Chełmno on the Ner some of the gravestones that she had discovered. It seemed to her that a lapidarium of headstones arranged in the Rzuchów Forest would be a good way of commemorating the past. There, she reasoned, lay the ashes of the descendants of those whose names were inscribed on the stones.

Jews from the surrounding localities were the first to be murdered at Chełmno on the Ner. They were brought to the palace there, supposedly to take showers. Then they were driven into the gassing vans. Once the motor was started, the exhaust gas flowed into the back of the van. This took place while the van drove the four kilometres to the Rzuchów Forest, where a team of Jewish workers buried the corpses in gigantic pits. Somewhere between 180,000 and 200,000 people died at Chełmno. Most of them were Jewish, although there were also more than 4,000 gypsies among them, and groups of Poles, Russians and Czech children from the village of Lidice.[1]

The Jews of Kole were murdered there during 8–11 December 1941. Part of the population of the Czachulec ghetto, where people from Turek *powiat* had been assembled, were also murdered there. The 1,100 Jews who had been crowded into the church at Dobra were taken to Chełmno on 10 December. Between 14 and 19 December 1920, people from Dąbie were taken there. The Jews of Krośniewice were taken to Chełmno in March, and those of Gostynin and Grabów in April 1942. On 27 January a letter was smuggled out and printed in *Morgenfreiheit*, an underground newspaper in the Warsaw ghetto:

> My dear,
> I have already written you one postcard about the fate that has befallen us. We have been taken to Chełmno and gassed: 2,500 Jews already lie there. The butchery goes on. Won't you have pity on us? Natan, the child, mother and I have saved ourselves, but no one else. What will become of us now, I do not know. I have no strength to go on living …

Only a few people survived the Chełmno death camp: Mordka, also known as Żurawski, Szymon Srebrnik, Michał Podchlebnik, Szlome Fajner and Abram Roj. The last two failed to survive the war.

Michał Podchlebnik, a Jewish saddler residing in Koło (4 Krzywa Street), testified on 9 June 1945:

> The first truck from Chełmno arrived at around eight

o'clock in the morning. The door of the van was opened, and a cloud of whitish smoke escaped. We were not allowed to approach the truck at that time, and we were not even allowed to look in the direction of the open door. I saw how the Germans hurried away from the van after opening the door. After three or four minutes, three Jews approached the van: Neumiller from Koło, Chaim Kiwer from Babiak, and a third whose name I cannot recall. They threw the bodies out of the truck and on to the ground. The corpses in the truck lay jumbled together and they occupied a space more or less half the height of the truck. Some had died embracing their loved ones ... and some were still alive. These were finished off by SS men, with a shot from a revolver, holding the revolver to their heads. After the corpses were thrown out of the truck, the truck departed for Chełmno ...

The corpses of my wife and two children, a boy of seven and a little girl of five, were thrown from the third truck that arrived in the Chełmno Forest that day (Tuesday). I lay down beside my wife's corpse and wanted them to shoot me. An SS man came up to me and said, 'That big oaf can still work well,' and struck me three times with a bullwhip, forcing me to resume working.

Łucja Nowak managed to recover some of the gravestones that stood in Turek cemetery before the war. She found the names of the former residents of the town inscribed on the stones: Pinchas; Aleksander, the daughter of Zelig; Jakub Kopel; Frajda, the daughter of Zew; Menachem Mendel; Natan Nate; Chenoch Henich; Cwi Hirsz; Zew Wolf. The names are preceded by: 'our teacher'; 'master craftsman'; 'rabbi'; 'venerated be his name'; 'he it is indeed'. But the most interesting thing, Łucja Nowak says, is the praise of the dead. We can read on the gravestones: 'Clean are his hands and heart'; 'Who walked the straight path'; 'Devoted to the Torah'; 'The crown on our heads'; 'He revered heaven and the truth'; 'His righteousness should be proclaimed to the world'.

The first mention of the Jews of Turek dates from 1798. Initially, they were buried only at the cemetery in Dobra. A Jewish cemetery in Turek is not mentioned before the 1830s. In his recollections of his childhood, Henryk Henoch Glicenstein describes an old, disused cemetery (this would indicate that by the 1880s there was already a new cemetery, probably adjacent to the old one). A mortuary and a lodging-house for poor travellers were built there. The cemetery was closed in May 1941 and, at more or less the same time, the grave of the Węgrów Rabbi, (who had died in 1937) was profaned. The complete destruction of the cemetery was carried out in 1943. In the State Archives in Konin, Łucja Nowak came across a document naming the institutions that were allotted gravestones for their use.

More than a dozen gravestones are left from the Jews of Turek. There are ashes in Chełmno, along with more than 24,000 spoons, about 4,500 pairs of scissors and 2,500 forks recovered from the ground. There are also a few survivors. And there are descendants, such as Miriam Gumpel, who came from Israel to see Łucja Nowak. Miriam's family on her father's side was named Zahn. Her mother was a Gołąb. Łucja Nowak found Joachim Zahn in the documents. He was a merchant trading in spices, silk and herring, and in 1938 he owned real estate worth 3,000 silver roubles, and had capital in the order of 2,100 roubles. Two years later, Joachim's real estate holdings were worth 7,200 silver roubles, and he had capital worth 4,000 roubles and a mortgage on the home of Karol Teodot. His son Mosiek was born in 1843, and his daughter Ewa in 1845. Joachim died in 1854. In 1863 the procurator applied to the mayor of Turek for the convening, at the request of a merchant from Radomsko named Fischl Winer, of a family council to act as guardians over Mojżesz and Ewa – still minors – the children of Joachim and Brajna Zahn. The application was motivated by the fact that their elder brother Abraham had illicitly taken full possession of the family property without making any provisions for the support of his siblings.

Dr Łucja Nowak found a birth certificate in the name of Chaja Frymel Zahn, the mother of Miriam Gumpel of Israel. There are other Zahns, such as Michał Zahn, who died in

1942; Sura Zahn Krotowski, who died in Chełmno with her husband (they were taken to the death camp from the ghetto in Czachulec); and Gitel Zahn, who died in 1902 and whose gravestone survives, as does the nineteenth-century grave-stone of Izaak Zahn. And then there is Ajzik Zahn – Miriam Gumpel's great-grandfather.

Miriam stayed in a hotel. She found several of her family's gravestones, so recovering a slender thread of memory. She took pictures and wept.

NOTE

1. Lidice was selected for reprisal killings after the assassination of Heydrich.

11 The Piano

A letter from Wanda W.:

I was found in October or November 1942 in Łuków, about 120 kilometres from Warsaw, after the departure of the Warsaw train. I was crying. All that remains in my memory is a nightmare connected with a suburban train. I said that one Mama had left and another would soon be coming. I was about three years old. I was small and thin, and dressed tastefully, with a bow in my fair, wavy hair, with blue-green eyes. A railroad man was standing in front of me. The Warsaw train was vanishing rapidly, and the station cashier had taken an interest in me.

The Sisters of Charity from Łuków, where I spent a short time, say that there was a card in my bundle, with a note written on it in imperfect Polish, reading: 'Good people, I am going off to labour in Germany, look after my child. Her name is Marysia Dobrzyńska, and she has not been baptized.'

I missed my mother badly at the orphanage, and spoke about a certain 'Majorka' – I suppose that this was a diminutive of the name Maria. I remember a large dog named Tumrze, and I also remember tall houses and trams. I spoke a pure, literary Polish at that time, and knew my rosary, but apparently I also understood Yiddish and even spoke a little, because there are recollections of this. The first thing I said in the home where I was taken after being christened was, 'Oh, a piano.'

I suspect that contact was made at that home with someone who could say more about me, since a great deal of the jewellery that I received as an adult was probably my own jewellery. And when I began my searching, my foster grandmother gave me her own ring and said, 'Remember us, even if you find a rich Jewish family.' The jewellery I was given was of Russian origin.

While they were still alive, my foster parents mentioned the cities of Lwów and Warsaw in connection with me. But they died suddenly when I was twelve, and I never learned anything concrete. I constantly played two games when I was little, and both of them were connected with my past, before the orphanage. I played a make-believe game about a domestic servant and her daughter. I always wanted to be that maid's daughter. I played a game about the arrival of a big brother named Jurek, who had stayed in Warsaw. I sang a prewar song about that brother: 'I'm a cold-hearted guy.'

I have very vague memories of someone showing an interest in me, more during the war, and only once afterwards. On two occasions, my foster parents handed me boxes of sweets. They had sad expressions on their faces. After the war, there was a little white celluloid elephant, stuffed with cotton. They never explained who those presents were from. But I was the only one who ever got anything. I had a little foster brother after the war and it surprised me that there were never any presents for him. There must have been something lodged in my memory about poisoning, perhaps the poisoning of my parents, because I began crying and feeling afraid when I came across an article about poison in the encyclopedia. And that's probably all that I can say about my childhood memories.

I have two children and four grandchildren. Like me, they have a marked gift for languages, art and literature, as well as a clairvoyant streak. Another recurring trait, at least in me and one of my granddaughters, is very strong baby teeth. That is, it was hard for the permanent teeth to come in.

How I would love to find a friend of my parents, at least.

Wanda W. lives in Poznań and Hanna Krall in Warsaw. They know each other through the Children of the Holocaust Association. Wanda W. wrote to Hanna Krall that she had been searching for her identity for years. She read what Hanna Krall had written in one of her books:

> The Polish parents of Jewish children are dying. They found those children fifty years ago along the tracks where a train ran, along a road where the Jews were marched, at the foot of the ghetto wall, or in the bushes. Sometimes they were given those children by people who promised to return, but who never came again. The Polish parents took those children to church. They gave them Christian names. They raised them as their own and remained silent about the past. Now, they are dying … In their last moments, they want to tell about it, but they speak unclearly about vague matters and die in the middle of a sentence. Others leave behind equally belated, indistinct letters, or scraps of memoirs.

Wanda W. knows even less about herself. Hanna Krall understands this, because she is a writer who writes about such things. She sent Wanda's letter to the journalist Marysia Tau, who lives in Tel Aviv. Someone might respond. Maria Lewińska, who studied with Hanna Krall at Warsaw University faculty of journalism, printed the letter in the Polish *Nowiny Kurier*. Under Wanda W.'s letter, she wrote, 'Spread the word about this letter, and perhaps someone will turn up who knows something about the tiny, frail, three-year old girl who exclaimed as she crossed the threshold of her new guardians' home, "Oh, a piano!"'

Hana Fajgenbaum understands Wanda W.'s pain. Hana Fajgenbaum lives in Tel Aviv, Her father, Szlomo, came from Warka. Lena, Hana's mother, was born in Warsaw, and her maiden name was Zajtman. Hana knows their dates of birth because she was eight when the war broke out, and unlike Wanda W., she remembers her parents.

91

Hana's story is complicated. It could hardly be otherwise, considering that she was in the Warsaw ghetto. She can still hear the screams. She remembers a cart loaded with dead infants and small children from the hospital. By that time, her father was already dead. Her grandfather was killed at Pawiak. Her mother was on the Aryan side. And then that cart drove up under the window of the house where Hana lived with her grandmother. Her grandmother finally said, 'Escape to where your mother is.' They passed her on to Zelwerowicz's daughter, who had a Jewish husband, Józek Nudelman, and helped children like Hana. Hana ended up with Mother Getter, a Franciscan nun. Then she went to Izabelina, and from there to Płudy. The Russians arrived. That was when she spent a whole night going to Izabelina on foot. She was looking for her mother. She met Father Oskar Wiśniewski in Izabelin. He was supposedly from Poznań. He looked Jewish and had also been in hiding, but Hana does not know if he actually was a Jew. She finally ended up in Cracow, at the JOINT building on Miodowa Street. She survived the pogrom. Her luck held – she was only beaten. She lost consciousness and woke up in jail. In 1946 she had no doubts – she had to get to Palestine. Her mother arrived seven years later.

Wanda W. spent only a short time with the sisters of charity, who quickly found foster parents for her. By the time the war ended, she had a foster mother and father, and many years passed before she began seeking 'proof of her own existence'. Hana Fajgenbaum, on the other hand, always knew who she was. When I sat in her apartment on Ben Gurion Street in Tel Aviv, relating the story of Wanda W., Hana said, 'I was older. I remember everything. I know who I am.' A nun from Poland was sitting there with us. She had come to attend a meeting of Jewish children rescued in Polish convents. Hana took us to visit her son. We entered that other house. I glanced at Hana. The look on her face was more positive. She hugged her grandson.

All this time, Wanda W. has been waiting for an answer. She wraps a shawl around herself, plays solitaire, and invites friends to visit her in her Poznań apartment. She tells people's fortunes with cards. She foretells the future. But she is still waiting for a pack of cards that would make the solitaire of her childhood come out. She would be grateful for one card. For a crumb of knowledge. For a few sentences. Just for some sort of sign ...

12 Wszawa Street

Someone has set the knocked-over gravestones of the former inhabitants of Koźminek back up at the protestant cemetery there. The gravestone of Leopoldina and Daniel Rosler, and that of Gotlieb Bencke, who died in 1904 and now asks that the passerby remember them before God. The gravestone of Maria and Karl Rajchert. On one of the graves, someone has placed a cross with the inscription: '48 German soldiers, German slaves, died here at the hands of the NKVD in 1945'. Somewhere nearby, with no marker, Sabina buried her younger brother Robert – a little Jewish boy.

Sabina is the daughter of Mendel and Abram Matusiak. She knows that her grandparents lived originally in Opatówek, and only moved to Kalisz after the birth of her mother, Hana. It was there, at their house at 19 Stawiszyńska Street, that she was raised until she was thirteen, until the day the war broke out. They called her grandfather Abram 'the short Jew-boy'. He spoke better Polish than Yiddish. He had a shop in Kalisz, traded with the Protestants from Katowice and was an observant Jew. On the Sabbath he went to the Great Synagogue on Złota Street, where he met Jechaskiel Lipszyc, the head rabbi of Kalisz. Lipszyc loved Kalisz so that even when he was offered the post of rabbi of St Petersburg and urged on by the Tzaddik of Gur himself, or offered Hamburg or Kaunas, he turned them all down. When Lipszyc died of a heart attack at the age of seventy in 1932, the Jewish populace went into mourning. Feuds and quarrels within the community stopped for several days. The Kaddish was said, and preparations made for the funeral. Abram Matusiak was one of those who went to pay his final respects to Jechaskiel. Among the mourners and rabbis from all over Europe who gathered at the old cemetery on Nowy Świat Street, he noticed Mendel Alter, the rabbi of Pabianice and the brother of the renowned Tzaddik of Góra Kalwaria. He knew that Alter was being groomed as the successor to Jechaskiel Lipszyc.

Customers were hard to come by because adults were out of work and many Polish and Jewish families were going hungry. In 1931 one-third of the Jewish families in Kalisz had no money to buy fuel for heating over the winter. The hunger was so great that during that year the Jewish community distributed 16,000 kilos of matzo among the poorest. In the mid 1930s, the Endek boycott of their shops made the situation of Abram and other Jewish merchants worse. Posters appeared reading 'Don't Buy From a Jew' and 'Go to Your Own for What's Yours'. Nevertheless, many poorer Poles retorted, 'Go to your own for what's yours, but go to Perl's for your shopping'. (Perl was a Jewish merchant with a vast warehouse and competitive prices.)

In August 1937 Dekert Square was divided into Jewish and Christian sections. As part of the Week of Propaganda for Polish Workplaces, the Endek hung a banner across the outlet of Kanonicza Street reading 'Kalisz without Jews'. It hung near the hardware store belonging to Hana's brother Zygmunt Matusiak, who had converted to Christianity in 1930. Outraged Jewish youths scrawled 'Kalisz without Endek Hooligans' on the walls of buildings and, under cover of night, Łajzer Kleczewski and Jakub Gelbart got rid of the banner on Kanonicza Street.

When war finally broke out, Mendel and Abram Matusiak fled from Kalisz to Widawa. Sabina recalls that there was still news about them in 1941. In December, however, the Germans deported some of the Jews from Widawa to the camp at Bełchatów. The rest were sent to the extermination camp in Chełmno in the summer of 1942, and the Jews from Bełchatów were sent there, too.

Sabina's mother was a beautiful girl. She was fourteen in 1924, when she met a handsome boy from Koźminek named

Bertold. He fell head-over-heels in love with Hana Matusiak. Young Berent had been a Second Lieutenant in Piłsudski's Legion. He came from a German family that had farmed in Koźminek or nearby for 400 years, increasingly coming to regard themselves as Poles. This is certainly why Bertold's mother acted as she did when the Germans entered the small town in 1939. When they suggested that she accept German citizenship, she replied: 'I am a Pole.'

Nevertheless, she did not want to approve her son's marriage to a Jew. When the war broke out, the situation grew more complicated. After all, everyone knew that Hana and Bertold were in love. Everyone also knew about their daughter Sabina (already thirteen) who had been living with her Polish–German grandmother since September. Yet the whole family was anxious about the fact that the Jewish girl was living there. They therefore placed her with Mrs. Maciaszek, who lived on Sienkiewicz Street in Koźminek. A carpenter named Kim stopped at Mrs Maciaszek's. He asked Sabina if she knew German and took her to his house. She had documents stating that she was Polish and was named Sabina Matusiak. So she came to work at Kim's workshop on Kaliska Street.

Sabina had no contact with the ghetto in Koźminek, which was surrounded by barbed wire. She knew that the local Jews, of whom there were more than 700 before the war, had been living there since April 1941. There were an additional 1,800 or so Jews, most of whom had been deported from Kalisz, in the ghetto. Approximately 1,000 Jews from Kalisz and Koźminek were exterminated in January or at the beginning of February. These were mainly children and the 'element unfit for work'. The Ringelblum Archive contains a letter sent from Kalisz by Moniek Gross to B. Lustig (at an address in the Warsaw ghetto). Gross wrote:

> I am so depressed by the misfortune that recently befell me that it is difficult for me to write. My beloved Parents were sent to the place from which no one ever returns again. They were sent along with two thousand unfortunates ... I do not know if you know everything, or if you are capable in the end of comprehending the enormous misfortune that has befallen our people ... I have

been working here for a long time as a cobbler in our workshops. I already know how to sew the uppers of shoes all by myself.

Mojsze Gross wrote his letter on 19 February 1942. His parents had been murdered at Chełmno several days earlier, and he was one of the last 150 Jews who were held in barracks on Wienerstrasse in Kalisz. On 4 July 1942, he managed with the help of Poles to travel to Germany as a labourer. He survived there until the end of the war, and wrote about his memories and the last moments of his farewell to his parents in *Książka Pamiątkowa Kalisza* (The Kalisz Memorial Book).

The remaining Jews were deported to the Łódź ghetto in July 1942. There were many cobblers, tailors, locksmiths, sandal-makers and electricians among them. The transport to Łódź included a group from Kalisz, who had been expelled from the city on 6 July. Mojsze Gross had been among them two days earlier. These people were given an hour to pack and assemble at the square in front of the station. At the same time, several hundred residents of the Koźminek ghetto were brought there. After spending the night at the square, they left for Łódź at 7.30 the next morning. Earlier, however, at one o'clock in the morning, 100 men and women had been sent to Inowrocław as labourers.

The transport to the Łódź ghetto included a fair number of Jewish children who had avoided deportation for many months, mostly by going into hiding. They had managed to stay on in Kalisz because there was no record of them. Yet finding hiding places for them was difficult. They were all put into four passenger cars. They had to leave their baggage outside when they got in. On arrival in the ghetto, they received quarters in the Central Prison. President Rumkowski visited and promised them work, food and clothing. Several days later, 39 more Jews arrived from Koźminek and four more came on 12 July.

Hana was in hiding at the Berents' building in Koźminek. There were four apartments there. In one of them, a secret passage, and concealed behind a wardrobe, opened into another apartment. Not a week passed without the Germans coming to enquire as to the whereabouts of

Sabina's mother. When she heard their voices, Hana slipped into the next apartment. She lived in fear, but with a man who loved her.

She became pregnant. On 23 August 1941 she gave birth to a son. Bertold named him Robert. He was proud to have a son, but the child was frail and sickly. They brought Dr Nurkowski to examine him in secret. Robert cried at night, and many people must have heard him crying. Someone may have informed, or perhaps people only wondered out loud how it was that there was a small child at the Berents'. 'One day,' Sabina says, 'just at noon, the Germans came into their home, leading father. "Where do you keep the child," they asked, holding a pistol to Berent's head. Robert lay hidden under a blanket. They found him easily enough. They ordered us to put on our coats. "Leave the child, at least," father said. "No, take that swine, too," replied a policeman. They took us to the police station. Robert was crying. They brought Nurkowski, but the child died in mother's arms. He was only six weeks old. His corpse was left at the police station. They took us to the Gestapo in Kalisz. They released me and ordered me to return to Koźminek, where I was supposed to bury my brother. The carpenter, Lange, made a little coffin and I buried Robert at the protestant cemetery. They sent Mama to Auschwitz. Father, for insulting his German blood, was put into the Sonenburg prison for three years.'

Sabina stayed at her grandmother's for four months. When she received a summons to report for labour in Germany, a policeman whom she knew warned her: 'I'm worried about you. Escape.' She took Henio Kajzer's advice and escaped from the transport near the oil refinery in Kalisz. She went up to a German soldier at the station and asked him to buy her a ticket to the village of Radlicze. She stayed there with a German family called Hornys, who were related to her father. When people started taking an interest in her, she returned to Koźminek and found Mrs Maciaszek.

Sabina's father died in 1976. She buried him at the Protestant cemetery in Kalisz. To this day, old people remember him: 'He was a good man. You could knock on his door at any time of the day or night. Even at midnight, he would harness up his horse if someone needed taking to the doctor's.' Sabina still lives in Koźminek, in the house that her grandparents built in 1903. The house does not belong to her today because the communist authorities confiscated it from her father. Sabina is a Protestant. She goes to confession on Good Friday and before Christmas. Her three sons, like her husband, are Catholics. She has no contact with Jews. But when old Bruks was still alive in Israel, she wrote to him. Bruks and his son Szlamek hid at the Kaponeks' in Słowiki during the war. They are probably the only ones from Koźminek who survived.

The synagogue and mikvah in Koźminek were converted into residential buildings, but one of the streets was named 'Heroes of the Warsaw Ghetto Street'. That's all. There is no trace of the Jewish cemetery, or of the barbed wire that surrounded the ghetto. All that remain are the tumbledown old houses where the Jews lived. And the memory of the residents of Koźminek, who still refer to Kiliński Street as 'Wszawa Street' (Lice Street).

13 From the Life of Mrs L.

You entered Abram Wolsztajn's salon through the front door of 26 Żydowska (Jewish) Street. In the hall stood a cabinet full of cosmetics. To the right were four chairs for gentlemen, and straight ahead two for ladies. There was also a cubicle for the manicurist. The clients were not only Jews. Poles who lived on the nearby streets and visitors to the fair also came here, as did local officials and merchants on occasion. Janowski, Wygodzki, Kronenberg and others. In September 1939 the Germans took Abram's salon away from him.

Abram Wolsztajn's daughter, Mrs L. recalls that her father was well liked. He did not flaunt his Jewishness. He played cards with Poles in the evening. Did he experience any unpleasantness from them? Probably not. The Polish pickets tended to march in front of shops. Or when a Jew in the traditional garb of a long coat drove in from Russian-occupied Congresb Poland, boys surrounded the coach and jeered the unfortunate newcomer. Mrs L. made friends with Polish girls. She made her first Jewish friend when she was in the commercial school. The girl was named Schleter. She lived at 30 Żydowska Street. It was only a few steps from there to Masztalarska Street, where Mrs L. lived with her parents.

Today, Mrs L. can recall only a few of the old inhabitants of that Jewish neighbourhood. Their neighbour Hirschlik had an excellent restaurant, and probably a bakery as well. When she closes her eyes, Mrs L. also sees the figure of poor Ćwierć, father of four, who ran a cheap café on the first floor of 26 Żydowska Street. She sees Levi standing there: a cheerful boy her own age and a real troublemaker, whose father – a kosher butcher – often chased him with a belt in his hand. Whole families are there. The Einsteins from 18 Kramarska Street: she was an outstanding pianist and her brother was a painter. The Skowrons, who had a dry-goods shop on Wroniecka Street (their grandson lives in Australia; he is alive because his mother saved herself by going to Germany as a labourer). The Wajnbergs from 6 Masztalarska Street – they were well-educated and went to Sopot for their holidays. The Ephraims, German Jews, had their millinery shop somewhere on Masztalarska Street. Through the mists of memory Mrs L. also remembers Serebryjski's café, but that family all died, supposedly.

Abram Wolsztajn, Mrs L.'s father, lit candles only at Yom Kippur. He was not a religious Jew and he lit them in order to summon up memories of his family. Mrs L.'s mother, Stanislawa, on the other hand, was a believer. They lived together at first without being married. When Mrs L. was born in 1918, Abram agreed to have the little girl christened. Why? Because Mrs L.'s mother was a goy.

It must have been a great love. She worked in Poznań town hall. She was a junior clerk. She had four sisters and a brother. One of the sisters married a Viennese man, and another a German (she left for Berlin with him in 1918). Her other siblings lived in Poznań.

Once, and that was still 'under the Germans', she was sent to Kalisz on official business. Lost and unsure of herself on a Kalisz street, she asked a young man for directions. The man was Abram Wolsztajn. It was probably at that moment, as in a good romance, that their feelings blossomed. Abram travelled to Poznań to see her. Later, when he knew that they would be together, he opened the hairdresser's salon on Żydowska Street.

When Mrs L.'s mother met Abram, Kalisz was a very Jewish town, and the community was classed as large enough to have a rabbinate. The head rabbi in those days was the famed Talmudist Jechaskiel Lipszyc. Although he was offered posts in Grodno and Lublin, Jechaskiel never left Kalisz. On the contrary, he must have loved the city very much, because after the First World War he was the first person from Kalisz to collect funds in the United States for the Kalisz Relief Committee.

The city came out of the First World War in very bad shape. First the Germans bombarded it, and then they looted the shops, warehouses and houses, shooting hundreds of residents. That was also when they burned the old Jewish archive. When the war was over, the Wolsztajns (only Abram's mother Gustawa was alive; his father Mojsze had died several years earlier) like all the Jews of Kalisz, set about rebuilding their old life. They organized a Credit Association, founded a Union of Jewish Craftsmen, and opened a library. Not everyone approved. Mrs L. supposes that her father must have been perfectly familiar with the events of March 1919, when unemployed people, who had been temporarily engaged in clearing rubble, demanded higher pay. They were joined in their strike by Jews from the Poale Zion (socialist) party. Endek thugs broke up the demonstration and then made their way to Wrocławska Street, where they looted Jewish shops. When the thugs returned to the Jewish neighbourhood the next day to continue the pogrom, they encountered organized resistance. Polish workers from the municipal gasworks turned out in support of the Jews. One of the thugs was killed, as were Mosze Anzel and Jehoszua Rozenblatt.

Mrs L. thinks it likely that it was the hard life of the Jews in Kalisz that made her father, Abram Wolsztajn, eager to move to Poznań. It was easier for Jews to stand on their own two feet and make their way there.

Had events moved differently, however, Abram Wolsztajn would never have opened his hairdressers' salon on Żydowska Street in Poznań. At the outbreak of the First World War Abram and his brother decided to escape to Canada as they did not want to serve in the Russian (Tsarist) army. Abram was unlucky, however, and was arrested and imprisoned. Later on, he met his future wife, and opened his salon at 26 Żydowska Street. His brother died, a bachelor, in 1930. The family inherited his property, and Abram used his share of the money to buy a car and expand his salon.

When war broke out for the second time, the Germans closed

most of the Jewish shops on 20 September 1939. Five days later they started to round up Jews. Mrs L.'s mother had had a brother serving in the Lwów Eagles in 1918. He fell in the fighting there and was buried in the cemetery in Lwów. So it was decided that Abram would be the brother, and not the husband, of Stanisława. Mrs L. had to learn to call her father 'Uncle Józef'.

Hirschlik, the Wolsztajn's neighbour, knocked on the door of their apartment on 10 December. He warned them that all Jews would soon be ordered to report to a camp on Główna Street: 'Get out, Abram.' 'I can't,' Abram said. 'It wouldn't be right for me, because I'm a city councillor. I have to stay with everyone.' Abram left for Warsaw at five o'clock the next morning. Mrs L. and her mother remained at the apartment in Masztalarska Street. The police came at noon. They did not allow them to take anything. They locked them in the synagogue, together with prisoners, not only Jews. They were held there for three days, then they were taken to Główna Street. The deputy to the German commandant was a Pole, Jerzykiewicz, a newsagent from Wroniecka Street. Abram had been a regular customer of his. They asked him for help. Mrs L.'s mother broke down and they both fell ill. In the end, they were taken to Mińsk Mazowiecki. Mrs Hirschlik, a Pole whose maiden name was Gawroniak, went with them. She later went to the Lublin district with her husband. She survived and returned to Poznań after the war.

They lived in Kotków, near Mińsk Mazowiecki. Mrs L. says, 'Mother remembered that the Kotlarz family was living in Warsaw. They were Jews who had lived in the same building in Poznań as the Lasmans. She knew that my father had their address, and might be there. She sent me to Warsaw on 20 December. The Kotlarzes lived on Muranowska Street. They told me that my father often visited them. They did not know where he was living, so I left our Kotków address with them. I started back towards the station and found myself on Bielańska Street, across from the chemist's. Some force compelled me in the direction of a door. I opened it, and there, before my eyes, stood my father. I returned to Kotków as if I had wings. Before two days had passed we were all together again. At first we slept in the Kotlarzes' kitchen. Later, we rented a room at 4 Muranowska Street. Preparations to set up the ghetto were underway, and they began building the boundary walls in April 1940. Muranowska Street was going to be inside the ghetto. Before the Germans finished walling off the Jewish district, we made our way to friends of my mother's in Cracow. We lived with them in a room on Krasińskiego Avenue. Several weeks later, we moved to Lubomirskiego Street. There we stayed until the end of the war, returning to Poznań in March 1945.'

Their home had been burned down, so they lived with Mrs L.'s mother's family. One day, they met Izrael Strauber, who had been hidden in a wardrobe in an apartment in Piekary for five years. Strauber was staying at the Jewish Old People's Home building on Żydowska Street. A Jewish committee was established in May, since more and more Jews were returning to Poznań. Wolsztajn and Struber travelled to Gdynia to collect UN refugee parcels. Shortly afterwards, Abram's family moved to a building on Żydowska Street that had housed a *Beit Midrash* (House of Study) before the war. They took an apartment on the second floor – above the apartment of Rabbi Sender, from whose family no one returned after the war.

In 1949 the Central Committee of Jews in Warsaw began cutting back on its activities. Its Poznań branch was soon closed down. That was when Mrs L.'s father went to work for Adam Rozenbaum, who ran a glass ornament factory on Koronkarska Street. Rozenbaum came from Łódź. He had moved to Poznań because he fell in love with a girl from Żydowska Street. They moved to Szewska after their wedding. Rozenbaum died young. Mrs L. remembers that they had two small children. Adam Rozenbaum's brother wanted to take the little boy to Israel, but Mrs L. cannot remember how all that turned out.

Abram Wolsztajn died in 1957, and Mrs L.'s mother, Stanislawa, in 1965. A film crew from Warsaw called on Mrs L. in 1997. They recorded her reminiscences for the 'Spielberg Archive'. Mrs L. agreed to meet them in a hotel. Why not at home? 'What's the point of starting the neighbours talking?' she explains. She does not want to talk about herself. She is afraid of prying eyes, pointed remarks, comments, things written on the walls ...

14 The Jews Return

'He would come to the office after dark,' Noach Lasman
recalls. 'He wanted to chat in Yiddish. He was a craftsman,
and he did not ask for anything or need anything. He came
from a small town in the Kielce region. He spoke Polish very
well, except, perhaps, for a village accent. He had survived the
occupation in Russia and had been a soldier in the First Army.
When the war ended, he met a girl, and they got married and
had children. He had a Polish name, so he did not have to
change it, as many Jews did then. His wife knew who he was.
She asked him not to say anything to her family. The man
agreed. But things hurt him deep down inside. That is why he
came to the Committee on Żydowska Street. Always in the
evening. Always in the dark.'

Noach went on: 'The lady came from Vilnius. She escaped
from the ghetto and stayed in hiding until, finally, she met a
young engineer at a forestry station in Byelorussia. She told
him the truth: "I am Jewish." They came to Poznań after the
war. They had several children. Unfortunately, the engineer
drank. Then he would beat the woman, heap abuse on her,
and harp on about her background. When he sobered up, he
would apologize. She used to come to the Committee to spill
her heart out. I saw the bruises on her,' Noach recalls. 'She did
not want to go to the police. She loved her husband. She did-
n't want to ruin his reputation.'

The police sergeant came from Podlasie. He spent the war
in Russia and came back to Poland with the army. He had
been raised in the Jewish community. He married a Catholic
woman. He longed for the past. He felt alienated, because he
could not go back to his *shtetl*. 'Perhaps he should have gone
to Palestine,' Lasman thought. But the old atmosphere of the
small Jewish towns was not to be found in Israel, either.

One day, the telephone rang. Noach heard the voice of a woman speaking broken Polish with a harsh German accent. She requested an appointment at the office. She came in several days later at the appointed time, with her son, who was dressed in sports clothes. The boy reminded Lasman of a certain local builder. The woman introduced herself; she had a 'von' in front of her last name. She confirmed the fact that she came from an aristocratic family. She said, 'My son's father is a Poznań Jew named Moses.' She said that she had come to seek help in arranging to emigrate to Palestine. However, she had no proof of the boy's paternity. She wanted the Committee to furnish the required papers.

The boy had always gone by his mother's name. His birth certificate read 'father unknown'. She had not been able to name the father during the war. That was reasonable. All the more so when the boy was drafted into the army. Although most of the Germans were evacuated from Poznań after the war, they had stayed. 'We had clear consciences,' said the lady whose name began with 'von'.

Lasman knew Moses only by sight. He remembered his shop on Nowa Street, near the Old Market. Moses was an old bachelor. He had frequently sued the publishers of the anti-Semitic newspaper *Pod Pręgierz* (In the Pillory). Noach had been unaware of Moses' rich erotic life. However, he could not fulfil the old lady's request. He promised to present the matter to the Board. They turned down the petition from the woman with the German accent. They suspected that she wanted to use the Committee to gain permission to leave Poland.

The Central Committee of Jews in Poland was established in November 1944. The country was divided into regions where provincial, district and local committees operated. When Jews began arriving in Poznań, a Committee was set up here. Lasman's job was to keep the files and the accounts, and look after the correspondence. He wasn't paid much. But the parcels of food and clothing arriving from overseas counted for something.

'The phone didn't ring often,' Lasman recalls. 'People would stop in from time to time looking for a certificate, an address, or help. These were usually people who had spent the war in Russia. Craftsmen told about going hungry. Those who had held party posts talked about the beautiful collective farms and gigantic factories. Nobody was lying, but everyone was speaking only a part of the truth.'

Noach could already see that being a Jew in postwar Poland would be very complicated. He recalls a woman about to graduate from agricultural school. She asked him not to come up to her on the street. She feared being recognized. She and her mother had survived on Aryan papers and now, she said, she 'did not want to reveal herself'. She told Noach that she had many suitors. Some were the sons of the Great Polish gentry. None of them knew that she was Jewish. She was afraid to mention it, because she knew about their negative feelings. As soon as she graduated, she told Noach, she intended to leave for Palestine with her mother.

Noach's most important duty was maintaining correspondence with the Central Committee of Jews in Warsaw. There were reports and surveys. 'I had the worst problems,' Lasman says, 'with supplying lists of the names of the people under our care.' He never knew who to put on such lists. After all, there were people who gladly accepted aid but did not want to reveal that they were Jewish.

Letters came from all over the world. People asked if anything was known about the fate of their families. They asked if any of their relatives might have survived. Occasionally, Lasman knew something about the fate of missing Jews. After all, he was from Poznań, and he knew them well. Someone once wrote that their family had been deported to Ostrów Lubelski, where the final *akcja* (action) was carried out in late 1942. There were also letters bearing good news. So it was in the case of Lasman's schoolmate, Olek. His family had fled to Nowogródek at the beginning of the war. He survived in a partisan band in the Nolibocka Forest. The rest of the family perished. Noach met Olek in Łódź after the war. And later, in the western zone of occupied Germany.

Letters sometimes arrived from America. They were written in German and addressed to the 'Jüdische Gemeinde in Poznań'. They contained requests that graves from before the First World War be looked after. This upset Lasman. He asked himself: 'Haven't they heard about what happened here?' Later, he realized that these people had surely heard that the Jews had been murdered, but they remembered the Germans as highly cultured people and did not regard them as capable of destroying cemeteries and synagogues. Or off killing *all* the Jews.

In 1946, or perhaps in 1947, the grounds of the Poznań trade fair were expanded. This was done at the cost of the old adjacent cemeteries, including the Jewish cemetery. Students were employed in the excavation. One of Lasman's acquaintances mentioned that while working they had found not only human remains, but also fragments of gravestones with some sort of 'hieroglyphics' on them. 'I knew what he was talking about,' Lasman recalls. He went to see the foreman, who confided that all the 'material' they excavated was being trucked to the old clay pits outside of town, where it was used as landfill. Noach brought this to the attention of the Committee. The Board agreed to write to the provincial governor. The governor asked for a meeting several days later. Noach made a presentation. He pointed out that this was not only a Jewish matter. 'It is barbarism to throw people's earthly remains into a clay pit,' he urged the governor. The Trade Fair administration should find the means to collect the remains and inter them in a common grave at the cemetery. The governor promised to intervene personally. Some time later, the symbolic funeral of the assembled remains was held at the cemetery, with the participation of the clergy. The members of the Committee received invitations to the ceremony,

In 1949 the Central Committee of Jews began cutting back on its activities. It closed down smaller branches such as the one in Poznań. The office was vacated and turned over to the Housing Authority. Lasman was out of a job, so he applied for a one-room apartment in the Committee's building. When they called him in for an interview, he said that he had lived in Poznań before the war, but that now he was alone. His family had all perished. He needed a roof over his head because he was working for a degree.

109

He was granted lodgings. It was the first time he had had a place of his own – in the former Jewish Old People's Home, at 15/18 Żydowska Street. Jewish Street. Before the war, it had been the Salomon Beniamin Latz Shelter Foundation for the Aged and Infirm. The merchant Latz had set up the foundation in 1847 as a hospital for impoverished pensioners of the Mosaic faith, above the age of 60. There were normally about 50 residents. The shelter contained 41 rooms and a library with access to the Yiddish press. A doctor visited twice a week, and meals were served five times a day. The residents were a few steps away from the *Beit Midrash* and the prayer house where they could thank the Lord for security in their old age.

15 The Good Pole

The apartment house stood at the corner of Żydowska and Dominikańska – Jewish Street and Dominican Street – a few steps from the prayer house. The building belonged to the community. Bronek Bergman's family lived on the ground floor: a poor Jewish family. They had a room with a kitchen and the windows looked out on to Dominikańska Street. On Friday evenings, Bronek and his brothers David and Gershon went to the prayer house, the one at the Jewish Old People's Home. One day Bronek saw a woman there who was 105 years old. Years later, he says that her face stuck in his mind and kept him awake for many nights. On Saturdays, they went to the Great Synagogue, the one on Stawna Street. They adored the Almighty (it was, after all, a religious family) and they kept kosher. 'Until September 1939, I never tasted *treyf* food and never failed to observe a single Sabbath,' recalls Bronek Bergman.

Rabbi Dawid Szyja Sender taught him religion. The rabbi was a young man with a joyful attitude. He detested begging. When Mr Zysman's business fell off, therefore, Sender said, 'Buy cheese and milk only at Zysman's.' Thus Zysman avoided having to beg. In 1938, after 11 years of marriage, Sender became a father. He could have divorced, but he waited patiently and the Lord heard him. During the war, the rabbi's wife and child were murdered. And Sender is said to have starved to death.

Bergman remembers the rabbi's large room in the prayer house. It was filled to the ceiling with books in Hebrew. In the middle stood a red plush armchair with its wooden frame covered in gold leaf. It had supposedly belonged to Rabbi Akiba Eiger. Yes, yes, the same Eiger whose knowledge so impressed the wealthy merchant of Leszno, Icyk Margolioth, that Margolioth offered his daughter's hand in marriage. When Bronek ended up in New York after the war and told the Hasidim there where he had been born, they burst out in exclamations at the sound of the word 'Poznań': 'Akiba Eiger! Akiba Eiger!'

His father, Pejsach, came from Widawa. Bronek visited the place several years ago. He met a local lawyer who gave him the manuscript of a book entitled *The History of the City of Widawa*. 'My surname is mentioned 65 times in that book,' Bergman says today. When he returned to New York, he went to the tabernacle of the Mormons, who are known for wandering from place to place to copy records of births and deaths. They had a copies of documents from Widawa up to 1850. Bergman found the name of his forebears there, as well. His cousin, who emigrated to Palestine in 1938, told him once that, according to family legend, one of their great-grandmothers welcomed Napoleon to Widawa when the army passed through on the way to Russia.

All that is left of the Jews of Widawa is one gravestone and a painting in the synagogue, which is still standing. Not much, considering the fact that the Jews setled there in the eighteenth century. At first, they belonged to the community in Łask. They set up their own independent community organization in 1838. At the outbreak of the war, more than 700 Jews lived in Widawa. When the Germans occupied the town, they burst into the rabbi's house and ordered him to destroy the Torah. Rabbi Mordechai Maroko refused. How did they expect him, a rabbi, to set his hand against the sacred book? He clutched the scrolls to his breast. So the Germans poured gasoline on him and set him alight. The rest of the Jews were deported from Widawa to Bełchatów and to the Chełmno death camp.

Bronek's father was a small businessman. He had a little shop on Kramarska Street, one of the many tiny Jewish shops on the ground floor premises of the buildings on that street. He sold tailor's accessories and blue silks. Bronek recalls that Mr Jakubowski, a neighbour from Żydowska Street, frequently stood in front of the shop. He had a purple nose. He was a penniless, kindhearted soul. He had no fixed employment, so someone paid him to stand in front of the shop and warn clients: 'Don't buy from a Jew.'

Bronek Bergman went to the school on Noskowskiego Street. Franciszek Stachowicz taught him Polish and history, and was his class teacher. All the boys had crushes on two girls: Bela Sędziejewska and Lucynka Abramowicz. Felek Lewkowicz was the best swimmer. The same Felek who was addicted to halva. Of his other schoolmates Bergman says: 'The older I get, the more often I see before my eyes Natek Zalc and Natek Tchórz, Felek Lewkowicz and Mulek Untermann, Jurek Janowski and Adek Redlich, Romek Rozenband and Izuś Braun, Jakub Schuchnerowicz, Heniuś Pakuła and Heniuś Badower, Bluma Zajdel, Jurek Herszberg and Nojuś Lasman, Maks Auerbach, Borys Mortkowicz and Heniek Kronenberg. Izuś Braun was the first to die. Supposedly for selling contraband cigarettes.'

It must have been 1 September 1939. Bronek remembers the Poles escorting people who were said to be Germans. They walked along Wielka Street in the direction of Chwaliszewo. Some of the onlookers picked up stones and threw them at those who were being marched along. Bronek recognized many faces among the Germans. Indeed, there were Jews who had lived in Poznań for centuries without ever learning to speak Polish properly. They felt a greater affinity for German culture and the German language. Poles regarded them as Germans. Bronek does not know what happened to those people. Then the Germans took the town, and the occupation began.

People bought everything that could be bought for money – even ragged thread. His father's dry-goods shop on Kramarska Street sold out in a single day. So Bergman spent all the money he had buying new material from the Wygodzki–Janowski firm. Once again, lines formed, and once again, he sold out entirely. The boom went on for several days. Then the Germans put a seal on the door and posted a guard outside it. 'What can I do?' asked Bronek's father. He had a shop full of merchandise. Fortunately, there was a back door, from the courtyard. When it got dark, the Bergmans moved all the material to the toilet, under the window. As soon as the curfew was over, they carried it all to their apartment on Żydowska Street. That was the end of the dry-goods boom for the shopkeeper on Kramarska Street.

'One day, SS men went up to the Jewish children playing in front of the Beit Midrash and started shoving and hitting them. They knocked my brother Gershon's head against the wall. Gershon fell to the ground, unconscious. He woke up in the municipal hospital. My father went grey overnight – Gershon was his favourite son. My brother survived the war, but he went stone deaf. I went to the United States in 1945 with him and my mother. My brother wrote a doctorate. He is a professor at an institution for the deaf. He has also written several plays.'

The Bergmans left Poznań for Łódź before the end of September. They had friends and distant relatives there. On 8 February 1940, however, police president Schafer issued an edict on the establishment of a ghetto. The Bergmans had to move to the Bauty district, where over 160,000 people were crowded into four square kilometres. Traces of other people born in Poznań, Konin, Turek, Kalisz and Koźminek can also be found in the *Chronicle of the Łódź Ghetto*, compiled in the Archive Department of the Jewish Council of Elders. One of them was Pinkus Ajzen of Konin, who knocked at the doors of apartments where Jewish officials lived and tried to convince their families that he had been sent to fetch food for their husbands, fathers and sons who were working late. The seamstress Rojzla Sochaczewska, from Kalisz, lived on Piwna Street in the ghetto. She died on Tuesday, 7 July, when the temperature soared to 42 degrees Celsius. She must have been exhausted that day, and perhaps that is why she fell under the wheels of a tram that crushed her skull at the corner of Marysińska and Mickiewicza Streets at two o'clock that afternoon. In a report by the police, we read that 39-year-old Juda Israel Julius, born in Poznań, was shot in November. We also learn that two residents of Koło, 72-year-old Gustaw Warbrum and 36-year-old Szajndl Gothajmer, were sent to the Central Penitentiary by the police.

The ghetto was located in the most run-down part of Łódź. Figures from the ghetto administration show that, out of 48,000 apartments, only 380 had indoor plumbing. The district was closed off by fences and rolls of barbed wire. A network of German sentry posts watched over the border with the rest of the city. Under an order of 10 May 1940, they shot without warning any Jew attempting to leave the ghetto without permission. Despite the great risk, the Bergmans took off their cloth badges and passed over to the other side of the barbed wire. They were smuggled from Łódź to Warsaw, where they lived with Bronek's father's sister. Their relative freedom ended soon, however. On 2 October 1940, Fischer signed an order for the creation of a closed Jewish residential district in Warsaw. The ghetto was closed off from the rest of the city on 16 November. That same day, an operation began to find Jews who were in hiding. The Bergmans moved into the ghetto, where they lived until October 1942. Bronek remembers terrible scenes. People were dying of hunger in the streets. They had swollen legs. – not their whole bodies, only the legs, because they had tried to relieve their hunger with water. Their legs became immobilized. At first, there were funerals. Later, the dead were collected from the pavements and streets, and buried like animals. Bronek remembers naked corpses being flung into pits.

He considers himself lucky because a distant relative arranged for him to join the sanitary corps. That is what saved his life in the ghetto. He went to the places where typhoid fever was taking the worst toll. At the time, he did not realize what dangerous work it was. 'Or perhaps,' he wonders after all these years, 'there was so much death around that the risk of contracting typhus made no impression on me.' The most important thing was that he had a cap bordered in red, and the Germans left him alone. After all, he was necessary.

Bronek's father lived on the Aryan side, where he rented half a kitchen. He got good papers for himself when they were still in Łódź, from a woman who helped Bronek's mother. Bronek's father asked her husband, 'Mr Krawczyk, why don't you report that you've lost your identity card and have a new one made?' Bronek says. 'That is how my father became Feliks Krawczyk, and I was his son Bronislaw.'

Bergman left the ghetto on a Monday morning by way of the courthouse on Leszno Street. He returned on Friday, carrying food. He gave bread to other people. Not all of them knew that he was Jewish. They thought that he had come to see acquaintances. They wondered why he would visit Jews when it was so dangerous in the ghetto. They called him 'the good Pole'. He was good because he brought bread to the Jews.

That dreadful day came. 'I remember it as if it were yesterday,' says Bronek Bergman. 'We were worried because father hadn't come home. He was usually back by that time. Suddenly, someone threw a wad of paper through the open window. We unwrapped it. Father had written: "The Germans are coming to kill you. Don't get into the train cars or on to trucks because that's certain death. I cannot get into the ghetto."'

'A truck drove up. The Germans shouted: "Everybody downstairs. We'll kill anybody who stays in their apartment." My mother said: "We're not going. Everybody hide in a different place." I ran up to the roof. Next door, there were Germans standing at the windows on the upper floors of the courthouse building. They threw something at me, shouting "There he is." I ran down to the courtyard. I opened the door of the latrine. I saw one of the tenants submerged in there and I jumped in. When the Germans looked in the latrine, we put our heads under. I was crouching – it was too shallow for me to stand erect. We weren't in there long. When we got out, the Germans were gone.'

Sara Bergman and her sons stayed in the Warsaw ghetto until October 1942. Later, they hid on Aryan papers. Bronek's father and his older brother Dawid died during the Warsaw ghetto uprising. Gershon had become a passionate reader from the time he lost his hearing. He disappeared. After the Uprising, it turned out that the Germans had put him in a camp for young people. Mother ended up in Pruszków. She had papers in the name of 'Zofia Mucharska'. They sent her from Pruszków to Germany as a labourer.

Bronek was with Doctor Jan Piwowarczyk in Częstochowa. He travelled from there to Cracow. He was arrested during a round-up and put in Montelupich prison. His origins were revealed in the showers. 'On our way back to the cells,' Bronek Bergman recalls, 'Kazik from Tarnów came up to me and said, "You f—— Jew." I was nineteen. I thought that was a death sentence. Another prisoner came up and said, "Give me your handkerchief because you're not going to need it any more." Night fell. I could not sleep. I kept seeing myself standing against the wall where they shot prisoners.

I feared the morning roll call. We were standing in double rows. The German commandant came along. They called him "March-March" because he repeated that word while kicking people. When the commandant was close to us, Kazik sneered "You Jew" and pushed me out of the row. That was a great infraction. The commandant went purple with rage. In an effort to save myself, I told him,"I am a German and I'm here by mistake. I want to be on the Eastern Front, I want to fight instead of sitting in prison." The commandant summoned a guard, and ordered that I be taken to his office.

I waited in the courtyard. A guard gave me a broom so that I wouldn't be bored. It was about 30 metres from there to the main gate. At a certain moment, the guard opened the gate to let a man in. He was showing him the way to the office. I saw that he had left the key in the lock. Without even looking around, I went up to the gate. I leaned the broom against the wall. I turned the key. I was on the street. I could feel my heart ready to jump out of my chest. I had trouble walking at a normal pace. In the end, I found myself in front of a building. I ran up the stairs to the loft.'

After the war, a Russian colonel helped Mrs Bergman and her sons sneak across the border. They lived in Berlin, Hanover and Frankfurt. They spent almost two years in camps. Next they went to the United States, where Jewish organizations helped them. At the beginning, Bronek dug ditches, for which he earned 75 cents an hour. He attended university classes in the evening, and eventually gained a diploma as a tax specialist.

Bronek has been coming to Poznań for several years. He walks down Żydowska Street, looks into the courtyard, and says nothing. He does not want anyone to notice his tears. One day, he told me, 'My real name is Baruch. Bronek is a name given to me by Zosia Kubiak, who helped my mother look after the children. That's what she called me, and it stuck. Many people know me as Bronek. But my father always called me Baruch. I am Baruch Bergman from Żydowska Street in Poznań.'

16 The Silk and the Knife

It is a beautiful house with a garden, in Tel-Aviv. Ester is playing the piano. We are looking through books about Poznań.
On a map of the city, we are trying to find the streets where
little Jurek ran with his friends. 'Oh, here's Wielka Street, and
this is where the Tanner's Dam was. Our home stood here.
When I ran to the school on Noskowskiego, somewhere
here'– he moves his finger over the paper – 'I would meet
Nojus Lasman, with a bag full of books, coming in my direction from Piaskowa.' Jurek takes out a photograph. 'Look,' he
says, 'this is my older brother Heniek and my mother in a boat
in Sołacki Park.'

His mother Cypora-Cesia came from Zawiercie in Upper
Silesia. There was a synagogue in her home town, and the
dead were buried in two cemeteries. There are still more than
a thousand gravestones left there today. The Jewish
Community offices were located in the Community building
on Marszałkowska Street. It wasn't far from there to the
Jewish Aid Bank. It was easy to find that institution, because
it was next door to the prewar Stella Cinema on Piłsudskiego
Street. When Ignacy Janowski moved to Poznań with Cypora
and his son in 1925, every fifth inhabitant of Zawiercie was
Jewish. Their second son, Jurek Janowski, was born the following year. A son of Poznań to the core.

The address of his father's new firm was: Wygodzki-
Janowski, Textile Manufacture Wholesale Shop, Poznań, 6
Wielka Street. Icek – Ignacy Janowski – was a talented merchant. That was why you could usually find him in the shop
on Wielka Street. On the other hand, Daniel Wygodzki, who
came from Tomaszów, had a wide range of acquaintances

among the entrepreneurs of Łódź. He was therefore the one who went to their factories to do the purchasing for the shop in Poznań. They had their own car. It was a Mercedes, which shows what a prosperous firm they were.

Janowski brought his brothers Mietek and Moniek to Poznań. They started out working in the business belonging to Ignacy and Daniel. Later, Moniek opened a delicatessen on Wroniecka Street. The daughter of Wolsztajn, the Jewish hairdresser on Żydowska Street, well remembers Moniek's wife: 'One of the most beautiful women in Poznań,' she says, although 60 years have passed since she used to go to the delicatessen on Wroniecka Street.

Yurek knew the letters of the alphabet when he was three. His father used to sit him on the counter of the shop at 6 Wielka Street. Clients would show little Jurek the mysterious markings, and he identified them unerringly. People said, 'What a gifted child.' Jurek could also read upside down. He was a prodigy at calculating. His parents sent him to school at the age of six. After several months, he was promoted to a higher grade. That is why he had already two years at the Paderewski High School when the war broke out.

He graduated from the elementary school on Noskowskiego Street. He walked there by way of Solna Street. He passed the barracks along the way, and the smell of the split-pea soup from the soldiers' mess still hangs over his home in Tel Aviv today.

The principal of the school was Mrs Propst. He remembers her crying at the school assembly when Piłsudski died. His teacher in the lower grades was Mrs Mornel. His class teacher was a Pole named Stachowicz, who taught mathematics. This teacher made Jurek stand up in front of the class to test his aptitude. Jurek had to do problems 'in his head'. He loved music class because he sang beautifully. He played soccer in Szelag, on the other side of the bridge. He did not enjoy school outings, however. 'A great pity,' he says, all these years later, because now he is a lover of nature. Back then, as a young boy, he missed out on a chance to appreciate the surroundings of the city.

'Good Lord, was I ever interested in sports,' he recalls. 'I would run to the Hotel Monopol, where the railroad school is

120

today, to hunt autographs. The players from LKS, the Łódź Sports Club, came to town. Romek Rozenband and I went to the Monopol. Romek looked very Jewish. We were trying to get Antoni Galecki's autograph. He was a defender for the Polish national team. We succeeded and went home thrilled. I went back to see Galecki again, and he said, "Don't bring your friend around any more, because I don't like Jews." Those words hurt. I went home. I took out a sheet of paper and wrote him a letter: "Our friendship is over, because I am a Jew, too." I mailed it to Łódź. A couple of weeks later, I got a postcard from Belgrade. I read it and could not believe my eyes. Galecki had written: "Don't worry, dear Jurek, everything's OK." And under his signature, the whole national team had signed their names. Before long, the Łódź team came to Poznań again. Galecki phoned and said, "I'll be at your place in a moment." Anoni Galecki met my parents. He told them, "Jurek has changed my attitude towards Jews."'

Jurek and his two brothers were sent to summer camp at Włodzimierz, near Łódź, in August 1939. They were supposed to fill in the gaps in their 'Jewish education'. Their father said, 'It will give you a better understanding of our culture.' In Wlodzimierz, Jurek met Icchak Kacenelson, a Jewish teacher and an outstanding poet. Icchak lived in Łódź and worked in the Hebrew school founded by his father, an authority on the Holy Scripture. Several years after the war, Jurek read his distressingly moving 'Song about the Murdered Jewish People', which had been buried in a bottle, under a pine tree far from Poland. It was a song about a handful of ashes, a cry rising from the inferno, an appeal from a lime-filled pit.

On 25 August his father telephoned. 'Your mother's coming to be with you, and I'll join you later.' They went to stay with a relative in Łódź, on 6 September; when people heard that the Germans were coming they began fleeing the city, hoping to escape eastward. That was the day when Jurek was awakened by the housekeeper's hysterical scream: 'The Germans are entering the city!' His father and older brother joined the refugees, while the younger boys stayed in Łódź with their mother. It was two days later, in the evening, that the Germans came. Hitler appointed Walther Blaskowitz commandant of the Łódź military district. The security police began arriving in town. Their chief, Reinhard Heydrich, had declared a day earlier that the 'gentry, clergy and Jews' in Poland should be murdered. On his way to the front lines, Hitler stopped in Łódź on 13 September.

For the first two months, no one knew whether or not Jurek's father and brother were still alive. There was no news. The boys felt safe with their mother as she was a resourceful woman. Jurek remembers how she wondered whether their apartment in Poznań had been plundered. She struck a deal with a truck driver and travelled to Poznań. She came back with five steamer trunks. One of them contained a knife that Jurek still keeps at his house in Tel Aviv. They were a wealthy family, and the things that their mother brought back from that trip enabled them to survive the war.

In the meantime, the Łódź police chief introduced compulsory labour for Jews. The Jewish community was required to supply 600 labourers for work each day. On 13 October the occupying authorities dissolved the community's board of governors and appointed Chaim Mordechai Rumkowski as head of the Jewish Council of Elders. A police battalion raided the Astoria Café on 1 November, arresting Jewish actors, writers and artists. Fifteen of these Jewish intellectuals were shot the following day in the Łagiewniki Forest. Jews were banned shortly afterwards from walking down Piotrkowska Street. On 11 November the police arrested the 30 members of the Council of Elders. Ten of these men were freed, with the rest being shot or sent to camps. The synagogue on Wolborska Street was burned down on the night of 16/17 November.

Mrs Janowska and her sons were already wearing the yellow cloth badges. They did not know what to do next. Cypora-Cesia felt that the noose was tightening around the Jews in Łódź. 'At last, a signal from my husband,' she rejoiced after a visit from a mysterious young man. The youth told her that he had just come back from Białystok. He had seen Jurek's father and brother there. They told the stranger that they were safe among the Russians. 'You are all supposed to join them. And take money,' he urged Mrs Janowska. She made up her mind. 'We're going.' They made their way to

Warsaw, and smugglers led them towards the River Bug by way of Malkinia. Mrs Janowska took an enormous quantity of baggage on the trip. They were supposed to cross at night.

'It must have been 30 degrees below zero that night. We travelled with porters. Suddenly, a Russian on horseback sprang up in front of us asking, *"Kuda idiosh?"* ("Where are you going?"). Then he shouted *"Nazad, nazad"* ("Get back, get back"). The porters with our baggage were getting ready to turn back. So were we. Mother began crying. In a flash, the same Russian was back. He asked Mother why she was crying. In that single instant, she understood that she had a chance. She told him that her husband and child were waiting for her. The Russian softened up and let us pass. We got as far as Siemiatycze. My father and brother were waiting there for us. When we stood face to face, Father asked, "Why did you come?" We were dumbfounded.

"I told that boy who visited you in Łódź that I wanted to come to you, not the other way around." It soon turned out, however, that this mix-up was to save the lives of the Janowski family. At present, however, Father was shattered. He was a merchant, and he could not engage in trade there. But Mother was more enterprising. She went back through the border to Małkinia and returned with the trunks that she had left there. She returned with silk dresses straight from Paris.

In May 1940 the Russians asked us, "Who wants to be a Pole, and who wants to be a Russian?" Whoever declared their Polishness became an enemy. At the end of June, they burst into our apartment. They gave us 20 minutes to pack, and then put us on a train that arrived in Archangelsk seven days later. Along the way, old Russians told us, "All that will be left of you is bones." Father and my elder brother were forced to work in the forest. Since I had a head for figures, they made me a bookkeeper. I calculated the volume of the lumber from the trees that were cut down. It was 40 degrees below zero outside, and I walked from one tree to another in every scrap of clothing I possessed. We must have been there for 12 months. When the Germans attacked Russia, they told us, "Go where you please."

That was when Father said, "Now our real trouble starts."'
They tried one city after another, but no one wanted to give
them any food. They were parasites, because they were not
working. They decided to go to Ulyanovsk. They lay down at
the station. 'The fleas were eating us up,' Jurek recalls. 'It was
Mother who saved us. She met wealthy Russian women. She
sold them dresses. She made friends with them. Thanks to
those women, we got a small room, and Father got a job in a
bakery. I used to go to see him under cover of darkness. I
would stand at the fence around the bakery. Father would
come out and throw me a hunk of bread. At last, we had our
fill of bread. I stopped dreaming about bread, and started
dreaming about margarine.

One day, I went with one of Mother's friends to a village in
the middle of nowhere. There was supposedly an abundance
of food there. I returned home with a full rucksack. It was, as
I recall, the middle of the night. Father got out of bed and
kissed me. He took a piece of bread and spread butter on it. I
will never forget that.

When Ulyanovsk was made a provincial capital, we had to
leave town. We travelled to Uzbekistan. We covered thousands of miles, ending up in the city of Kokand, in the Fergana
Valley. The palace of Khan Hudoyar was there, and Kirghizis,
Uzbeks, Tadzhiks and Kazakhs walked the streets. It was
dreadfully hot. There were thousands of refugees. Filth,
typhoid, hunger. We lived on dried apricots. My youngest
brother was the first to fall ill, but he got better. Then my
father fell ill and died. Then my brother Heniek came down
with a stomach typhoid. He too died. There was no medicine
and he died in terrible agony. I was left with my mother and
younger brother. The fact that we were vaccinated was not
the only reason we survived. My father and older brother
were honest, and all they knew how to do was work. But in
Russia, you had to know how to steal, bend the rules and
avoid the hardest labour in camp. There was no other way to
survive.'

Before they could return to Poland, they had to resist
attempts to make them accept Soviet citizenship. But Jurek
Janowski said, 'I'm a Pole.' He was thrown into prison. He
stayed there for five weeks. He never accepted a Soviet

passport. The Russians were furious and confiscated all his family photographs, which he never recovered. They finally released him. The Janowskis returned to Poland by way of Lwów. They crossed the border in January 1946. Only then did they learn that their whole family, numbering some 100 persons, had been murdered. Jurek's father's brothers, Moniek and Mietek, had perished. Moniek's wife Maryla came from Łódź, from the Pilcewicz family, who lived on Zachodnia Street. They went to Warsaw when war broke out, and soon found themselves in the ghetto. When the Germans rounded up the children, their son was taken away. Izio was sent to Treblinka in one of the transports. Maryla is said to have gone out of her mind. She ran around the streets of the ghetto looking for the boy. She also died at Treblinka. Moniek is said to have taken his own life. Mietek, Jurek's other uncle, had a wife from Kielce. That is where they went when the war broke out. Nothing is known about what happened to them.

The Janowskis learned that their home in Poznań had been destroyed. They went to live in Wrocław. One day, Jurek ran into Pola, who had been his older brother's girlfriend in Russia. She gave Jurek a photograph she had received from his brother. It showed Jurek's brother, Heniek, with his mother. They are standing in a boat.

After the Kielce pogrom, they joined the Germans who were being deported. They found themselves in the West. Jurek got a job with the Americans. His knowledge of the language came in handy. He had learned English in Kokand. His younger brother, Stefek, went to Munich to attend school. He had an obsession about learning things.

They travelled to Israel from Marseilles by ship, disembarking in Haifa. Jurek came under the care of an aunt who had emigrated from Poland before the war because she had nothing to eat. Jurek studied and served in the army. He met Ester in 1955. She was a beautiful soldier who was born in Radomsko, Poland. He liked her, and used to run into her on his way to work each morning. They got married. Ester had two children: a daughter Semadar (the name means flower of the grape vine) and a son Oren (pine tree). Jurek Janowski was an economic consultant and a university employee. He travelled to many countries as a consultant to the Ministry of Defence.

After arriving in Tel Aviv, his younger brother Stefek lived in Haifa with an older, childless couple who had announced their readiness to take in a survivor. He finished school, went to university and became an engineer. When they started building an atomic facility on the sun-scorched steppe at Dimona, he took a job there. He wrote letters of application to American research institutes, got a scholarship at one, and went there. He was only going to stay for a year but he has been living there now for four decades.

Jurek Janowski has visited Poland three times. He does not have any bad memories of his homeland. He remembers that he lived well in Poznań. He survived the war in Russia, leaving the graves of his father and brother there, and he returned to find ashes in Poland.

When he came back to Poland the first time, he felt as if something was crushing his chest. It scared him. He called Ester and said, 'Fly to Zurich.' When they met, he could not stop talking. From morning to night. Ester listened patiently to Jurek's stories and his memories of Poland.

17 An Ordinary Life-story

Jurek was in the Łódź ghetto from February 1940 to July 1944. He spent barely ten weeks in Auschwitz, between August and November 1944. He was in Braunschweig from November 1944 until February 1945. and in Watenstedt from February to March 1944 (five weeks). From there he went to Ravensbrück from March through to April 1945 (five weeks) and then on to Wobelin from April until 2 May, when he was liberated.

In some ways, his is an ordinary story – one of many thousands of Polish Jews. The only thing that upsets the logical and well-planned course of events is the fact that Jurek Herszberg survived, in spite of the intentions of the Nazis.

We are standing on Jackowskiego Street. It is August, early in the morning. We stand looking at *that* apartment building. A head in hair-curlers leans out of a third-floor window. We crane our necks and the hair-curlers disappear. As we scan the ground floor of the building, the hair-curlers cautiously re-emerge. So it goes on, back and forth. While I keep observing the hair-curlers, Jurek cannot take his eyes off a ground-floor window. I know that, in his mind, he is wandering around the apartment of his childhood. At this moment, he may be in the kitchen, talking with his mother, Gustawa. Perhaps he and his sister Ania are waiting for their father Lajzer to come home. He can smell the coffee, and their maid, Pelasia – his 'second mother' – is just emerging from the servant's room. It is 1939. On 18 May Jurek has just turned ten. He is already a man, and can pray with the other men in the synagogue.

'Behind the door on the left was the children's room,' Jurek says. Next to it was my parents' bedroom with its lovely balcony. On the right-hand side of the hallway were the dining room, the kitchen and the little room for the servant.' The Herszbergs were the only Jewish family in the building.

At first, Jurek went to the school on Noskowskiego Street. But that was some distance away, so his parents transferred him to a primary school nearer home. Jurek remembers that, when the children said, 'Saint Theresa, pray for us,' he did not have to recite those words. He had several Polish friends, and they sometimes walked together to school. But the boys always left him alone when they reached the front door – they did not want people to say they were Jew-lovers. One class-mate he remembers is Zbyszek Tomaszewski, who played the piano beautifully. He remembers a couple of little girls: Jasia Graczyk and Ola Nawrot. (He had a crush on them!) Jurek was short, no good at soccer and had little chance of attracting the attention of girls, for whom the fact that he was the best at maths hardly counted! On the other hand, his father appreciated his abilities, and would sometimes take him to Hirschlik's restaurant, where Jurek played chess against grown-ups. Afterwards, on the way home, his father was proud of his little son.

Jurek was only at the movies once before the war. He saw the animated version of *Snow White* at the Sun Cinema. And he ate pastry at the Esplanada Café once. 'You don't forget a moment like that as long as you live,' says Jurek Herszberg, 'because I was there with my father, in the better days, when we lived on Jackowskiego Street.' Lajzer Herszberg was then a sales representative for Oskar Cohn's firm, the Widzew factory. He lost his job during the depression. They became a poor Jewish family, unable to afford to rent an apartment in an upmarket building. So they moved to Chwaliszewo, where they lived on Czantoria Street. His father took it hard and died in 1939, just before the war. Jurek remembers going to the synagogue to recite the kaddish for his father. He remembers reciting in a trembling voice: '*Yizkor Elohim nishmat mori ...* '

His parents came from Łódź. Until the age of eighteen, his father was a strictly observant Jew, but this changed when the family settled in Poznań. The synagogue stopped being so important. Of course, they still observed the most important Jewish holidays at home – especially Yom Kippur. For what Jew, even if he doubts what he learned in *cheder*, could remain hostile to the Lord on that day? 'And additionally,' Jurek admits, there always remains in man that grain of doubt. You ask yourself: What if God really does pronounce his verdict on that day? Perhaps He writes down the *mitzwes*, the merits, and *hatuim*, the sins, in the Great Books. Perhaps it is precisely on Yom Kippur that He proclaims the verdict.' Since no one could be sure one way or another, the synagogue in Poznań on Yom Kippur was filled with even those Jews who observed rarely or not at all during the rest of the year. Like Lajzer Herszberg, they went there and gazed at the gold, silver and copper many-branched candelabra, and at the candles placed in them, each of which had its own flame. Each one was different, pale or darker, rose-coloured, red, blood-red, or bluish. They cast their light on the Aron-ha-kodesh that stood behind the azure balustrade, reached by semi-spiral stairs at the sides, and on the lions, embroidered in silver thread, that supported the tablets of Moses. It was so dark that when little Jurek looked up from his place in the men's section on the ground floor of the Stawna Street synagogue he could barely make out the great cherubim and the 12 arcades painted around the lower edge of the dome, symbolizing the 12 gates of Jerusalem.

What he remembers best about the Łódź ghetto, where they fled after leaving Poznań, is hunger and the taste of a hunk of bread. That bread led to an unending succession of criminal cases, such as the one against Szlama Arager in March 1941. Szlama's crime was concealing the corpse of his 7-year-old son in order to go on using his food ration card. The rumours that constantly circulated in the ghetto were enough to drive people to despair. It was said that those without work would be sentenced to starvation and would receive only 80 grams of bread per day and 20 grams of sugar per week. They would be excluded altogether from the distribution of potatoes and vegetables.

The atmosphere was dreadful. People kept dying or disappearing. No one could be surprised at the fact that there were many suicides. Icek Pinkus Kopel hanged himself in his apartment on Berka Joselewicza Street. Rubin Starozum hanged himself in the attic doorway. Erich Siegberg swallowed

Luminal tablets. Gabriel Frydman, an insurance agent, jumped from a fourth-floor window in a building on Młynarska Street. Transports kept going off into the unknown. The day finally came, as late as July 1941, when Jurek was among the people herded into the square that served as an assembly point. He stood among hundreds of Jews with suitcases. His sister Ania was with them, but not their mother, who had died in the ghetto. They were forced into cattle-trucks. The journey lasted a long time. When the doors of the cattle-truck were opened, they were in Auschwitz. He was separated from his sister, and he remembers that Ania began to cry. 'Look after yourself,' he called to her. He was sure that they would meet again in two or three hours, for he did not yet know that he was in a death factory. The moment of parting haunts him to this day, because he never found out what happened to Ania. He was luckier. He went 'in the right direction'.

He spent ten weeks at Birkenau, for he did not have a number or a striped camp uniform. After several days there, he met up with someone he knew – Menachem Kupferger. Menachem was a strong boy, and he showed off his muscles when the Germans came looking for some men for labour. After several weeks of labour, they killed Menachem. Jurek, by contrast, was short, slightly built and frail – not suited for work. At first, he lived in Barrack No. 14, but soon volunteered for a transport. He mentioned a name at random and found himself in a cattle-truck. They were taken to Braunschweig where he worked on trucks, cleaning screws. 'I was always lucky when it came to light work,' says Jurek, 'otherwise, I would never have survived.' Twenty weeks later, he was transferred from Watenstedt, and from there to Ravensbrück, where he no longer worked. The only thing that prisoners did in that camp was die. Those who remained alive only waited for death. Jurek finally ended up in a small camp in Wobelin, where the Americans liberated him on 2 May. Somebody said that the prisoners should kiss the boots of their liberators, but this proved to be impossible. They stood there, filthy and lice-ridden, and at a considerable distance from the American soldiers, who found it easier to chat with the SS men. The SS were clean, shaved and in well-fitted, neatly pressed uniforms. However, the Americans gave the prisoners soup and bread. One of them said to Jurek, 'Go back to Poland.' So young Herszberg crossed the Russian lines and started back for Poland.

When he was on his way back to Łódź, they asked him at the border where he was going and where he had lived before the war. The Polish soldiers said, 'You speak Polish well, Jewboy. But what are you coming back for? Poles live here.' Jurek could never forget those words. He admits that he had expected something better. He thought that someone at the Polish border would say, 'Welcome home.'

He reached Łódź on 15 June. At first he slept at the station, then he found the building where his aunt, Izabella Nowacka, used to live. Someone told him that they thought she had survived and was living in Tarczyn. He tracked her down. It was an emotional moment for her. He had no idea what to do next, so he went back to Łódź, where his friend Paul Gast talked him into going to Prague. He remembers that that was when he stopped being afraid, for he knew that he could stand on the street in Prague and that no one would kick him. He would not hear the contemptuous phrase 'Jew boy'. He learned that there was an assembly point in Terezin for Jews wishing to emigrate from Europe. He went there, but it turned out that he did not fit in with any of the other groups: not with the religious groups, not with those who wanted to go to America and not with those on their way to Israel. He kept saying, 'I want to study mathematics.' So in the end they sent him to London, where he studied, gained a doctorate in algebraic geometry and then became a university lecturer.

'The fact that I survived is of no particular interest,' says Jurek Herszberg (a mathematics professor from London for whom the smile of another human being means more than a thousand books). 'I was no hero. I never ran away. I never took up arms and fought. I was nothing more than a child of the ghetto and a prisoner in several camps. Why did I leave Poland? Because the air is different here.'

18 There's Nobody Here Anymore

When Henryk Kronenberg gets off the train at the station in Poznań, his wife Krystyna is afraid that his heart will burst.

An apartment in a corner building on Langiewicza Street appears in Herst (Henryk) Kronenberg's earliest memories. It is 1925 – a sweltering summer. Little Henryk walks with his friends along the banks of the River Warta. He helps chase a neighbour's cow. On one occasion, he grabs a horn, clambers on to the animal's back, and rides across to the far side of the river. Henryk had a friend called Juju, who came from a Protestant family. He raised pigeons. He gave a pair to Henryk, who hid them in the loft. That was where Henryk experienced his first love, with Pelasia. She helped him feed the pigeons. She asked, 'What will you grow up to be, Henryk?' He replied, 'A tram driver.' She laughed and said, 'Be a doctor. It's so much more fun.'

The years of puppy love ended. Cows and pigeons gave way to notebooks and ink. Henryk's Jewish school occupied a big red-brick building, still standing, on the corner of Szewska and Stawna Streets, a few steps from the Jewish orphanage and the new synagogue.

Henryk walked from the Wilda district to school by way of Półwiejska and Szkolna Streets. Then he passed the pillory that stood in the Main Square and slowly made his way into Żydowska Street (Jewish Street). On his left was the Jewish Old People's Home and the *Beit Midrash*, while on his right was the building where the Bergmans lived. Henryk was friends with their older son, Bronek.

'When I close my eyes, I see the little buildings, streets, shops, people,' Henryk Kronenberg recalls. The Sun Cinema, the National Economy Bank, Dobski's elegant café. Students belonging to the ONR (the National-Radical Camp) once hung a sign on the door of Dobski's reading 'Dogs and Jews Not Allowed'. Dobski took the sign down. The students put it back up. Dobski took it down. Then the students came inside the café. They occupied all the tables. They ordered soda water and, sipping it slowly, sat there all day long. Dobski capitulated. The sign stayed on the door.

'Skinny, grey-haired, not very good-looking. We called her "the old lady",' says Henryk Kronenberg. 'So many years have passed and I can still see her standing there with an armful of books and notebooks. Mrs Propst was the principal of the school for Jewish children. She taught us to love Poland. I remember how she loved literature. Thanks to her, I said, "I am a Pole of the Mosaic faith." It's incredible that there were people like that.

Some of the older pupils belonged to Hashomer Hatzair, a Zionist organization. It was clandestine, because Mrs Propst was opposed to Zionism. She used to say, "You are citizens of Poland. Don't think about Palestine. Your homeland is Poland." When the war broke out, the boys from Hashomer Hatzair wanted to hide their banner. They sewed it up into a couch cushion. When Mrs Propst noticed it at the Sonnabends', she said, "Perhaps you were right to raise your children to think about emigrating to Palestine." I've heard that the banner was packed into a metal box and buried somewhere in the Szeląg district.

He had a great influence on me. I first met him when I was eight or nine. I went to summer camp in Inowrocław, and Izio Sonnabend was in charge. He lived in the same building in Poznań that the school was in. We used to meet after lessons. Izi once told me, 'We are citizens of Poland, but our nationality is Jewish.' He put me in touch with Jurek Rein, who became my first Hashomer Hatzair leader. The next leaders of the group that I belonged to were Felek Mornel, Zali Sieradzki, Michał Kolski, Stefan Szlechtarz, Ernst Bauer and the phenomenal Jakub Lissak, known as "The Little Fox". Jakub was born in Koło in 1916. His parents moved to Switzerland in the 1920s. They later returned to Poland, to Poznań. They lived in the Łazarz district. "The Little Fox" joined the organization later than most. He was intelligent, hardworking, and a good speaker.

There were two of us Jews in my class in secondary school: Saluś Mordkowicz and me. The senior Jewish boy was Witold Szuldit, two years older than us, an orphan who grew up in the home run by the Workers' University Association on Wielka Street. He dropped out of school in 1936 and went to fight in Spain.'

One of the teachers Henryk remembers was named Szulczewski. He wore the Sword of Bolesław the Bold, the emblem of the nationalists, in his lapel. He was tough, but fair. Henryk's class teacher was Fuks (a name that means 'green-horn). When a student made the smallest mistake, Fuks dictated a note to his parents: 'I am never prepared for my Polish lessons. Please punish me and impose tighter discipline.' Stefek Zimny, the son of a policeman and gifted at drawing, was a specialist in forging parent signatures.

When Kronenberg's mother went to the school for the first time, Henryk suggested that she might like to have a talk with Fuks. She agreed. She went into the teachers' room and said, 'Mr Fuks?' The teacher praised her son's progress at school. But next day he came into class and slapped Henryk across his left cheek and his right cheek, and then led him outside into the corridor. 'What's my name?' he said. That was how Henryk learned that 'Fuks' was a nickname, and that his Polish teacher's real name was Piotr Jankowicz.

Once Henryk overheard older people talking about the enchanted lions that stood in front of the Opera. They said, 'When a virgin walks past, the lions roar.' He wanted to hear them roar, so he invited Basia G. to meet him on the opera steps. 'We sat on those steps for hours,' he says, 'and no matter how many female students passed, the lions remained still. It was there, on those steps, that my heart began to beat faster.'

He was not religious. When the time for his bar mitzvah came, a teacher from Kalisz was engaged to prepare him. 'I'm not going to study,' Henryk told his parents. 'I don't need a bar mitzvah.' His parents were tolerant, and accepted this declaration equably. Mama only went to the synagogue for the Kol Nidre on the eve of Yom Kippur. Father said, 'You can decide for yourself when you grow up. Just keep the Ten Commandments.' His grandparents were unaware of all this and sent him a bar mitzvah present – a watch. He was the first boy in his class with a watch. They also sent him prayer requisites.

He fell in love at the age of sixteen. Instead of playing truant, he would go to the Raczyński Library with his girlfriend, where they would read poetry together. That was when Henryk stopped going to Hashomer Hatzair meetings. Things remained this way until November 1938, when many Jews were expelled from Germany. 'This is wrong,' he told his girlfriend, and returned to the organization. For a month he delivered warm clothing and undergarments to Zbąszyn.

His sister began attending the Dąbrówka secondary school. The girls exchanged presents on St Nicholas day. When Halinka and her Jewish friend unwrapped their presents, they found only garlic inside. Henryk remembers thinking, 'There's nothing for us here. We have to build ourselves a country in Palestine.'

In April 1938 several members of the Poznań Hashomer Hatzair went to Kalisz to take part in Hachshara at the kibbutz there. Many Zionist organizations were represented. The young people from Poznań found many acquaintances from Włocławek there and quickly felt at home. The Hachshara members left Kalisz on the first day of the war. Henryk recalls: 'The Hashomer group included Zalus Mordkowicz, Fredi Bauer, Gustaw Fajngold, Jurek Harsztark, Lutel Cyruliczak, Adaś Tasiemka, Lowa Sochaczewski, Józek Szop, Rafi Sonnabend, Ismar Glasman and Natek Dukielman. There were also girls: Fira Sochaczewska, Ania Milewicz, Benia Braun, Rutka Lewin, Reginka Winter, Niusia Kirszenbaum, Renia Moszkowicz, Genia Ickowicz, Sala Chrzanowicz and Irka Wermus.'

The Hachshara was set up in Kalisz by Hashomer Hatzair in 1931. It was called Hechalutz Hashomri (Scout Pioneering). The organization prepared young people to work in Palestine and also ran a summer camp for about 120 children each year. Hashomer instructors acted as camp counsellors. Another

Zionist youth organization, Hechalutz Hamerkazi (Central Pioneering), was also active in Kalisz. It prepared people for agricultural kibbutz work. There was Hachshara at the nearby Jewish agricultural estate in Barczysk. Many *halutzim* (pioneers) emigrated from there to Palestine. The leaders were Jakub Grinszpan, Naftali Ziego, Chaim Sztajn and Josef Engel.

When the war broke out, Henryk Kronenberg was near Pińsk, in the middle of his military training. He wanted to get back to Poznań. But how was that possible, when everyone was heading in the opposite direction, eastward? He fell into the hands of the Muscovites in mid September. He refused to accept a Soviet passport (after all, he had just recently sworn his allegiance to the Polish Army), so they kept him in the prison at Pińsk until May 1940, and then sent him to a labour camp.

He lost contact with everyone. Years later, he learned that his family had fled from Poznań to Warsaw at the beginning of the war. His Uncle David, who was fairly well off, rented them an apartment on Żelazna Street, but they were soon in the ghetto. Henryk's father died before the Jewish uprising, when it was still possible to have a funeral. (Henryk is still searching for his grave.) His mother was deported to Treblinka and his sister Halinka to Majdanek. From Tola, a woman from Poznań who was in love with his Uncle David, he learned that Halinka had been a teacher in the ghetto. She taught Polish to the Jews.

After the war, Henryk Kronenberg came to Poznań. He walked Stawna, Dominikańska and Szewska Streets like a stray dog. One day a man came up to him on Żydowska Street and said, 'I know you.' 'Where from?' Henryk asked. 'You used to go to Hashomer Hatzair over there.' 'Yes, I did,' Kronenberg replied. The stranger introduced himself: 'I'm Marych.'

Marych was the king of the local youth gangs. With hope in his voice, Kronenberg asked, 'Did anyone survive?' Marych said. 'There's no one here anymore.' And then he added, lowering his voice, 'I was a trusty in Auschwitz. I helped save Izi Sonnabend. I saved Lowa Sochaczewski.' Henryk did not believe him.

He decided to travel to Łódź. First, however, he went to Marych's for dinner. Marych was living in the old people's home on Żydowska Street. After dinner, Marych walked him to the station. He said something to the conductor, and the conductor took Henryk to the compartment where the train crew sat. When he reached into his pocket a moment later, his fingertips brushed against a small flat bundle there. He waited until he was at the Łódź train station to unwrap it. It contained 10,000 zloty. When Henryk had got himself back on his feet, he travelled to Poznań to repay the money, but could not find Marych. Neighbours said, 'They caught up with him one day.'

Henryk Kronenberg emigrated to Israel in 1957. His cousin phoned him one day: 'Henryk, come over to my place. Izio Sonnabend's here from Australia.' Henryk recalls: 'I walked into my cousin's apartment and asked Izio how he had survived. He answered, "Marych saved me." Later, Lowa Sochaczewski came to visit from Switzerland. "Henryk," he said, "I owe my life to Marych from Poznań."'

19 Testimony

'My husband Dawid Hofnung and I left Poznań several weeks after the Germans occupied the city. Jews were already being shot in Fort VII. Benno Rindfleisch, Juliusz Tychauer, Eliasz Czak, Pinkus Gojner, Szul Zylberberg, Zygfrid Juda, Bertold Junter, Eliasz Junter, Herman Junter, Abraham Aron and Dawid Glanternik of Kórnik, and Eryk Golland of Buk died there. We went to Łódź, but living conditions there were terrible. We therefore took refuge in Warsaw, where we lived in the Praga district. When the ghetto was closed off in November 1940, we moved in with relatives of Dawid's on Smocza Street, which intersected with Stawki Street, where the Umschlagplatz, from which the deportees left, was located.

We made our living at the time from the sale of bicycle parts. They were supplied to us by my brother-in-law Godlewicz, whose business was still open (he had a Polish woman as a partner). This was not a bad business. Bicycles and rickshaws were then the primary means of transport in the ghetto and in Warsaw. In those days, I frequently went to the Aryan side to pick up merchandise. Although I took off the armband with the Star, I was frightened because it was easy to fall prey to extortionists.

I lost my sister Lola in the first operation, in the final days of July 1942. A German threw her into the sewer during a round-up. She spent nearly two days sitting there, up to her neck in filth. She got out, washed, changed her clothes, and was caught again and placed on a transport to Treblinka. I remember the children marching on to Umschlagplatz, led by Janusz Korczak, during the first liquidation operation. That was when I took my little niece out of the ghetto and on to the Aryan side, where her parents were. The Jewish district was reduced in size after the liquidation operation, and the border of the ghetto, which was now a vast labour camp, ran along Smocza Street. Employees of the workshops belonging to Fritz Schulz and Kurt Rohrich lived in the buildings on Smocza.

My brother Natan was then working at a quarantine centre outside the ghetto. He supplied me with papers in the name of Adela Łagun. My husband obtained papers in the name of Kazimierz Drzewnicki. From then on, we always passed ourselves off as an engaged couple. We found an advertisement offering a room for rent in the *Nowy Kurier Warszawski* (New Warsaw Courier). It belonged to a certain woman residing at 27 Wileńska Street in the Praga district. Our landlady did not know that we were Jewish. We lived with her almost until the end of the war. Initially, we were helped by my brother-in-law. He had Aryan papers and went on trading in bicycle parts along with his Polish partner. Someone informed on him in 1943, and he was shot. Godlewicz was probably regarded as a very wealthy individual, and they must have demanded a great deal of money from him. The Domański family in Białystok took his daughter in. I remember that I often went to church with her. The priest once said from the pulpit, during his sermon, that butter was so expensive because all of it was being bought up by Jews in hiding.

Fortunately, we 'looked good', and no one suspected that we were Jewish. Once, however, a policeman called on us and demanded a large sum of money to remain silent. Since we did not have so much money, we agreed to pay him in monthly instalments. There were times when we had no money to pay the policeman, and then we hid in other Warsaw apartments. One of the places we hid was with Bronek Bergman, who went by the name Krawczyk during the war. We also ran into an alcoholic extortionist who demanded money. He was satisfied when we gave him a watch and a violin. I remember sometimes hearing it said on the street during the ghetto uprising that the Germans were finally clearing the Jews out of Warsaw.

When the next Warsaw uprising took place, the Russians entered the Praga district and we were free. Then our landlady learned that we were Jewish. She was unhappy about this and, on one occasion, whilst under the influence of alcohol, she came right out and told us, "I regret having given you shelter." We moved out and lived nearby in Grochów until the end of the war. After liberation, my husband went to Białystok to get our niece from the Domańskis. He found her and brought her back to Warsaw.

We emigrated from Poland in 1950. We lived with our niece in Ber Sheva, where Dawid worked as a secretary for Histadrut. Unfortunately, he died two years later. I then moved to a kibbutz and remarried. My son Menachem is a lecturer at the Hebrew University in Jerusalem. My niece lives in Rehovot and is a painter.'

Lea Zolty (née Leosia Gerson)

20 Butter on a Leaf

In the ghetto I used to say, 'God is in Berlin.' From the camp, I remembered the taste of a piece of dry bread and of potato peelings. And also that children must always walk with their mother between them. Fate was kind to us. I survived, my brother and sister survived, my mother survived. That's a lot, but not so much that I do not long for my father too.

My parents met in the Ukraine. My mother was Rachel Sznejer and my father was Hersz Sochaczewski. Theirs was a great love, and they had to flee to independent Poland in 1920. But I, Fira Sochaczewska, and my brother Lowa managed to be born in Russia. Father decided to cross the border into Poland when Lowa was several months old. He took along his mother-in-law and my mother's sister. At the border he said that they were his own mother and sister. When the whole pack of us reached Łódź, it turned out that my father's two 'real' sisters had died (one of them in childbirth). But my grandparents were alive in Zduńska Wola, and in fairly good shape. They rejoiced at our return. My father, a weaver by trade, opened a millinery shop in town. One night, he was burgled. 'Now what can I do?' he asked in despair, looking at his wife and children. Mother had relatives in America, and Father in Berlin. They wrote to him, saying, 'Hersz, come and live with us.' Nevertheless, he had made up his mind: 'I'm staying in Poland.'

After the First World War our parents were looking for a place where they could build a new life for themselves. Like other Jews, they had escaped the *shtetl* and moved to the big city. They wanted to give their children a good education and they talked about assimilating and blending into the Polish landscape. That was why my father, Hersz Sochaczewski, began doing business in Poznań in the early 1920s. After several years he decided to settle there for good. We moved there in 1926, when I was seven. We lived first at 12 Szewska Street, in an apartment building that is no longer standing. We rented a room from the Segals, German Jews, because it was hard to find an apartment of one's own. That building stood across the street from the Jewish primary school which I attended for the first three years. My teachers there were Mrs Propst, Mrs Mornel, and Mrs Kantorowicz. Mrs Propst had a backward son – a boy who suffered from depression. I had no contact with him. Mrs Propst was a strict teacher. Once, one of my classmates and I laughed during the singing of the Polish anthem. She came over to me and said, 'You're not allowed to laugh during the Polish national anthem.'

Some time later we moved to a four-room apartment at 18 Kozia Street, with windows looking out on the Old Town Square. (That building is also gone now.) Father opened a wholesale work-clothes outlet at 3/5 Wielka Street, on the second floor, and Mother helped him with the business.

In primary school, and later in secondary school, they took a dim view of Zionist organizations. One of my classmates, Benia Braun, who lived on Stawna Street, was expelled from school for that reason. We had been assigned to write something about workers, so Benia described the workers who were building Palestine. They kicked him out. In the meantime, we were searching for new directions and new ideals. We found them in the Hashomer Hatzair organization. Our goal was to emigrate to Eretz Israel. That is why we taught ourselves the history of Zionism, read about Soviet collective farms and formed study groups. When Hitler came to power, we looked fearfully at what was happening in Germany. Many of my friends managed to leave Poznań and Poland before the war. Those of us who still lived there went to school, to the theatre, to the opera, to the cinema. We spent our summers at camps organized by Hashomer Hatzair. We met young people from Włocławek, Kutno and other small towns. Life in Poznań went on in its own sleepy way. We had it good. Our parents were merchants, craftsmen, lawyers and doctors. In general, we lived well, and there was no poverty among us. From time to time, we scheduled a lecture. The lecturers spoke in Hebrew and Yiddish. Jabotinsky honoured one of those meetings with his presence. He gave a political speech. We listened to him without enthusiasm.

At the end of secondary school, I registered in the commercial school. They accepted me without an examination because of my good grades. Some of the teachers said that the school was 10 per cent Jewish, and that that was too much. They treated me in a friendly way, nevertheless. There were three other Jewish girls in my class: Ida Milewicz, Hania Auerbach and Renia Kirszenbaum. We went on excursions together. I was in Gniezno once. I must have been very silly because I was afraid to go into the cathedral. However, I broke the wafer with others at Christmastime. Our class sponsored a poor family living in Naramowice.

I used to see a handsome young student on my way to school. We always passed each other at the same time. When he got close to me, he would bow politely. One day, I walked to school with Hania Auerbach. Hania had frizzy hair and Semitic features. The student stood there thunderstruck. He did not bow, but only said, 'Do you enjoy the company of Jews?' He was offended at me and began acting as if he did not know me. One day, completely by chance, I happened to notice him and his friends writing 'Poland for the Poles' on the wall of a university building.

I had, in fact, already found love. Ten years earlier. He was Heniek Winter and he lived at 11 Szewska Street. We went to the same secondary school. He was very poor and had no father. I used to lend him my school textbooks because he had no money to buy any for himself. He sometimes came home with me for supper, and one summer Mama invited him to join us on vacation in Puszczykowo. We were terribly shy and if either of us put a hand on the other one's shoulder, we were ready to die of fright. We never kissed. Heniek went for Hachshara. He ended up in Russia after the outbreak of the war, and died there.

It was the last vacation before the outbreak of the war. Idziek, Lowa, Heniek and Rutka from among my group of friends went away for Hachshara. Others were supposed to join them, but the atmosphere was terrible. We had a large group of Jews in Poznań who had been expelled from Germany in 1938. We took them into our homes. My parents took in two solitary Jewish men whose families were in England. One of them, whom we put in the nursery, was named Schlesinger. Our apartment was full of talk about what Hitler would do next. We lived with a foreboding of war.

I spent the vacation in Krościenko. There were a handful of people from Poznań there who were older than me. That was when I took my first independent steps in adult life. I met new people. The world seemed beautiful to me. It was a very hot summer and I returned in the last days of August to find the stations packed full of people, the trains running irregularly and the ticket-sellers with no change. I barely made it to Poznań. I asked myself, 'What's going on? Has the war already started?' No, that was impossible. I reached Kozia Street a week before the mobilization. There was panic in the city and people were buying up foodstuffs. I got up to go to work on 1 September, and my father told me, 'The war has broken out.'

The Poles arrested many Germans. They accused them of cooperating with the aggressor. I remember meeting a group of those who had been arrested on Freedom Square. People were throwing potatoes at the Germans. Our fury knew no bounds. Then I noticed my boss, Zygfryd Kohn, among them. He was a German Jew. I felt stupid and went away.

The Germans entered the city ten days later. We had a party at my parents' apartment. We covered the windows with blankets, and Lutek Cyruliczak brought delicatessen items, wine and sprats. We told ourselves, 'As long as we're alive, let's live it up.' Lutek joked, 'If I mix together two wines containing 14 per cent alcohol, I'll get a drink with 28 per cent alcohol.' We were very young.

Germans whom I knew said, 'They won't allow the Jews to stay here.' But the Germanized Jews in Poznań felt sure of themselves. After all, they had their medals, and they had fought on the German side during the First World War. At first, only Poles were expelled. However, my father was uneasy. He said, 'I'm going to Zduńska Wola. Things might be better for us there.' I went with him. We found Germans there. Father looked around and said, 'This is such a small town that everybody knows me. Let's go to Łódź.' Things were also disturbed there. Jews had been shot and arrested in cafés and on the streets. Father consoled himself, 'There are so many Jews living here that Hitler will never be able to do anything with them.' We rented a four-room apartment, and the rest of the family joined us, along with Father's sister, Bronia Warszawska.

They issued orders to move into the ghetto. We got a room with a kitchen. Sixteen people were quartered there. Father went to register with the ghetto administration. 'I'm from Poznań,' he announced proudly. He was a very handsome man, and he must have made a good impression because we were assigned a place.

Things were very bad in the ghetto. We used up all our reserves, and there was no one we knew among the Poles on the Aryan side. The introduction of ghetto money made smuggling or trading at the ghetto wall impossible. We had no jobs. One day, my father saw an announcement on a wall: 'Men needed for work in the former Jewish district.' They were needed to demolish the walls, in which money and jewels were supposedly concealed. He and Lowa went to apply for jobs. Since my father was the oldest one there, they told him, 'You'll make coffee.' Lowa picked locks and padlocks. My sister and I got into a firm that sewed sweaters for German airmen. Only Mama had no job. (She was already past fifty.) By some miracle, we arranged to find work for her in the gypsy camp, but after three days, she said, 'I'm never going back there again.' She had seen terrible things there and did not want to tell anyone about it. She ended up working alongside me. We were in the fortunate situation of having no children or elderly people with us who could not work and would therefore not receive food rations. Each of us got bread and a portion of soup. Father and my brother got additional portions of food at work. At first, each person received two kilos of bread per day, 100 grams of meat per month, and a small amount of potatoes, sugar and flour.

I was promoted to office work because I knew bookkeeping. That was when I met Chaim Rumkowski. He ordered them to send me from the office back to the production line. He believed fanatically in 'salvation through work'. He faithfully carried out all instructions from the German administration. He made the ghetto more productive and kept setting up new workshops. When there was a selection, he protected those capable of working, at the cost of the rest.

Zyson, the boss, followed his orders and kicked me out of the office. He waited until Rumkowski had left, and then put me behind a desk again. There came a time when Rumkowski ordered him to provide a hundred people for a transport. The boss told me, 'Dear child, I'm going to keep you, but I have to give up some others – your mother and sister.' I begged him to help us. He gave in, and decided to deceive the Germans. The last page of the list was glued on, and that is where the names of the Sochaczewskis were. It was agreed that the last page would not go to the Germans. But first I had to play out a scene of despair in front of everyone, begging Zyson for mercy, so that no one else would suspect the deception. We did not manage to keep my close friend Stefcia Rezlich. At first, we thought of hiding her. But those without jobs got no food ration. Stefcia decided to travel into the unknown. None of us knew at the time that the trains went to Treblinka, or that there was a death camp there.

The son of the Łódź textile mill owner, Maurycy Silberstein worked in the office. Because he had been a student in France, and I came from a commercial school, Silberstein bridled at the fact that he and I were paid the same. I took his place when he missed work for several days, and it turned out that I knew just as much as he did. From that day on, he began to look on me with more respect, and then he finally proposed to me. I told him, 'We're not going to get married amidst this filth.' He answered, 'In that case, I'm going to volunteer for deportation. I can't go on living like this.' He went to the assembly point on Czarnecki Street. He received a loaf of bread and some marmalade. I went to say goodbye to him. Mother shouted, 'What are you going there for? It's dangerous!' It was 1944 and transports were leaving each day. I found him. He was wearing shoes with holes in the soles, because he was ashamed to march in clogs. They had just brought in a group of workers from Poznań who were no more than skin and bones. The sight of them terrified him. He was lucky, because just that day they called off the deportation and he went home, arriving late at night. But now we had to leave our district. We went across the bridge to the other part of the ghetto, but there was no work there, and no food rations. The ghetto was dying. People said, 'Pack up the machines, we're going to Bavaria.' We had to live in one room – eight of us. We made a hiding place because we did not want to leave the ghetto. One day, two women with little children came to the room. The Jewish police were on the stairs, right behind them. It was too late to hide them. They took us to Czarnecki Street – my father, my mother, my brother, my sister, Silberstein, and me – with our possessions in little bundles. There they loaded us into cattle-trucks. We travelled for three days before arriving at Auschwitz. We got out of the cattle-trucks. It was night. A light was burning. There were people in striped uniforms speaking Yiddish. 'Isn't this just lovely,' I said to myself.

Auschwitz was hell. Shouts of 'To the left!' and 'To the right!' Gunfire. German shepherd dogs with their hackles up. A boy sneaked up to us and said, 'Mr Sochaczewski sent me. I'm supposed to check that you're with your mother. He says: "Take care of her!" Somebody started beating him and he ran away. I asked a German, 'Where are our menfolk?' He replied, 'If you work, then you'll get to see them.'

He cut bread for us, because we had no knife. In return, we gave him our watches. On the unloading ramp, he asked how old Mother was. I lied, saying, 'Thirty-nine'. He waved her through. Then came another selection. They stripped us naked. They took Mama away. I did not know what was going on. They shaved us. My sister said, 'You know German. Go and ask them to give Mama back.' I went up to a German. I was naked. It was a terrible feeling. I said, 'Give us our mother back, she's stronger than we are.' 'Go get her yourself,' he said.

Mother was standing there naked, with her shoes in her hand. She weighed 39 kilos then. Perhaps she already knew what lay in store for her. I gave her my hand and led her away from the group that was on its way to the gas. That was when my sister and I decided that mother would always stand between the two of us. We got through the next selection. There were several girls with us whom we knew from the Łódź ghetto. In all, there were ten of us. We were happy. That was when a *capo* came up to us and asked, 'What are you so joyous about?' I answered, 'You're looking at a mother and her nine daughters.'

My father and brother remained in Auschwitz and met two people from Poznań there. Leon was both an intellectual and a drunkard, but a good man even in camp. The other was Marych. As soon as he saw my father, he began weeping and gave him a loaf of bread. Marych was a child of the streets. He lived on Żydowska Street and defended us when we had problems. He was not a thug. He sometimes came to see my father. When he was hungry, he got a zloty for bread. Marych was a *capo* in the camp. He said, 'Mr Sochaczewski, get out of this place. Get out as fast as you can …'

They decided to send us to Bremen, and so loaded us into cattle-trucks – 300 Jewish women from the Łódź ghetto. In Bremen, we found 500 Jewish women from Hungary who were already there. We got a hunk of bread, coffee and soup in the evening. Our hair grew back, and we managed every once in a while to find a few potato scraps. I was very frail then and could not always lift my spade.

Bremen was bombed. They ordered us to march. No one knew where we were going. We reached Bergen Belsen several days later, where they shoved us into some sort of building. Hell could not have been worse. It was night. There was a dreadful stench. I went outside in the morning and all around were corpses that had been rotting for several days. That was where the smell came from. Orders were given. Four women were supposed to bury a corpse in a hole that they dug themselves. I did not have the strength. For the first time, I saw that sand could move. A terrible thing. There was nothing to eat, and there was typhus. We went seven days without eating and without washing. Whenever anyone wanted to go to the toilet, they never made it, because it just came bursting out of them. The camp was liberated on 15 April. They still managed to hold a roll call that morning, during which they confiscated our bowls and blankets. 'There won't be any more food,' I told my mother. 'I'm going to throw myself onto the wires. I don't want to live any more.' My mother held me by my dress. She would not permit me to go. So I went into the barracks. 'I'll die here like a dog,' I said. Around noon, I heard some words in English and French. The Allies did not enter the camp; rather they photographed us from a distance. They threw cans of food and cigarettes through the barbed wire. Many people died from that food. I remember a dead woman with an open can in her hand. They were lying in the ditches, in the field, in front of the barracks.

We emigrated to Sweden in a Red Cross transport. My brother Lowa joined us several months later. We had relatives in Sweden. My father's brother had settled there in 1905. He came to Poland before war broke out. He never managed to return to his family. He died in Otwock. We found their address in the telephone book. It was a joyous meeting, and I found pictures of my parents and grandparents there – the only documentation of the past. We lived in Sweden for five years.

Lowa told us about the way that he and Father had gone from Auschwitz to Dachau. My father had died of typhus, as had Silberstein. That was when I recalled how my father had always been an optimist. A rabbi had told him that there would be no accidents in the family and that we would all die of natural causes. The rabbi was wrong. Father's whole family died in Berlin. His brother died in Warsaw. His second brother died in Otwock. His sister and her children died in Chełmno. The only one who survived was his uncle from Berlin, who had emigrated to Argentina before the war.

149

A handful of us Jews from Poznań, us Jews from Poland, remained. It is natural that I dreaded going back to a country where pogroms were staged even after the war. Yet I never forgot it, the same way that I never forgot the taste of the butter wrapped in leaves that mother used to buy from the Poznań farm women.

We left for Israel in 1949. My brother Lowa stayed in Sweden. We lived in Ramat Gan. At first, I did not tell my children about what I had lived through. But the past cannot be erased. Do you know that my husband, Mendel, had been an Auschwitz prisoner? He has a number tattooed on his forearm. One day a lady came into my husband's business and said, 'My daughter is afraid to come here because they said in school that the only Jews who survived were those who pushed others out of the way, who trampled on corpses as they fought for their own lives. And the good Jews died.' It hurt – words like that inflict wounds.

When my son turned six, he asked us, 'Mummy and Daddy, buy me a bicycle.' I told him, 'No, I'm not going to buy you a bicycle. I did not live through the war and the camp just so I could stand at the window now and worry that you'll get run over by a car.' He answered, 'So, just because you survived the war, I can't ride a bicycle. I think there's something wrong with you.'

21 Chaim's Shoes

Chaim Mordkowicz was a respectable Jewish craftsman with a bootmakers' shop at 45 Wielkie Garbary Street. The Mordkowiczes had three sons: Zaluś, Szmulek and Borys. Zaluś, the elder, was the spiritual leader of Hashomer Hatzair before the war. Intelligent and quick-thinking, he impressed the young Jewish people.

When the war broke out, the Mordkowiczes did not flee the city. The Germans came in and shut down the Jewish shops and businesses. At the beginning of December, the Jews were told to assemble at the camp on Główna Street. They came with their bags packed. They were placed in barracks, and then loaded into cattle-trucks three days later. They rode in these wagons for several days. They realized from the stations they passed that they were travelling eastward. Like most of the people from Poznań, they were thrown out of the train at Brzeźnica. They made their way to the little town of Ostrów Lubelski. They did not feel at ease in that small locality. 'Perhaps we would be less noticeable in a large city,' they told themselves, and decided to go to Warsaw. They spent the winter in that city. The spring came, and with it letters from old friends in Poznań. 'We are in Łosice,' wrote Taub and Abram Lasman. 'Come join us here, and it will be easier for us to see out the war together.' The Mordkowiczes accepted this invitation and went to Łosice with their sons. At first, it was tolerable there. They worked building a railway platform, draining marshes and repairing roads.

A ghetto was opened on in Łosice on 1 December 1941. It covered only a small area and the sanitary conditions were horrible. An epidemic broke out and people starved. Several months later, Zaluś travelled to the camp in Siedlce with Noach Lasman. In late August, the boys received a letter from the Mordkowiczes: 'Get out of there. We must save ourselves.' They returned to Łosice. They began looking for a suitable hiding place and a Pole agreed to shelter them for a suitable fee. They had to hurry as it was known that the Germans were going to liquidate the ghetto soon. They made it just in time. They left the ghetto on 22 November 1942. Five days later, the Germans surrounded the closed district and sent everyone there to Treblinka.

In the ghetto Chaim Mordkowicz had continued to make shoes for German and small-town Polish dignitaries. There were always several pairs of shoes, paid for and ready to be collected, in his workshop. When the escape from the ghetto had been prepared down to the last detail, Chaim stubbornly insisted on leaving the finished shoes behind. Zaluś and Borys wanted to take them along. 'Why should they fall into the hands of the police?' they asked their father. 'If we are caught, those shoes will not make help us, but they will not harm us, either. We will be killed one way or another.' But they could not convince Chaim. 'The fact that other people steal does not mean that I must act the same way,' he said. An argument flared up. That was when Mrs Mordkowicz intervened and said, 'Chaim will not change his principles simply because fate has brought him together with murderers.' So the boots, labelled with names, stayed behind in the workshop. No one knows whether they reached the murderers. Someone may have noticed the Mordkowiczes leaving and plundered the workshop first.

The potato cellar measured six metres square and belonged to a Polish farmer whose farmhouse had burned down. The peasant took the risk in exchange for solid payment in gold coins purchased before the war. The Mordkowiczes, their sons, Noach Lasman and the Perelman brothers from Łosice all lived in the potato cellar. They stayed there until August 1944.

They were saved by the fact that the Mordkowiczes knew about dreams. One day, the peasant told them, 'Run away, because my wife had a dream in which the Germans surrounded our farm and shot everybody. Now she's very frightened and doesn't want you here any more.' The boys wanted to go to Józef's wife and convince her that dreams are only a superstition, but Mrs Mordkowicz said, 'No. I'm the only one who knows how to talk with a peasant woman.' So she went to Józef's wife and told her that she could disregard the dream. She said, 'We Jews are a venerable people and we know how to use the Bible to interpret dreams.' In the Babylonian book of dreams, she explained, fire is a harbinger of good luck. It worked, and the peasant woman agreed that they could stay in the potato cellar.

Once the war was over the Mordkowiczes lived on Gdańska Street in Łódź. Zaluś and Borys went to Germany. Their parents stayed on in Poland. Their apartment was a stopping-off point for people coming back to Poznań. Mrs Bergman and her son Gieniek showed up there, and Icek Ickowicz, the Redlichs and the Hazensprungs stopped there on their way back from Russia. Their apartment was also a place for farewells. When the Lasmans emigrated from Poland in 1957, they travelled to Łódź in the mistaken hope that they could persuade the Mordkowiczes to join them. The Mordkowiczes refused on the grounds of Chaim's health.

When Noah Lasman was living in Israel, he was sent on business to a certain country in Africa. Mrs Mordkowicz wrote a letter to him while he was there. She called him irresponsible. 'How can a man with a wife and small children travel to a wild country?', she said. She worried as a mother. Noach wrote back, 'Dear Chana, in this "wild" country, I met a man who stayed with you in Poznań for several days before the war and made friends with Zaluś. He was a diamond merchant. His name was Herman. He came from Włocławek and he belonged to Haszhomer Hatzair.'

Chaim Mordkowicz died in 1971. Chana then agreed to travel to New York, to her sons. She was then almost 80. They put her in a lovely nursing home in the Bronx, on the banks of the Hudson. Noach Lasman visited her one day in 1977. She was happy to see him, and as they walked around the old people's home, she kept introducing Noach as her son. Lasman says that she had every right to do so. Noach's son Marek came to visit her a short time later. She said, 'Marek, my grandson.' She died in her sleep. She did not suffer. After all, God knew what she had been through.

22 *The Times of our Youth*

'I packed in secret. I left my suitcase at a friend's. Only one of my sisters knew that I was leaving. The day of my departure for Grodno came at last. There, at the other end of Poland,' says Ida Milewicz, 'the young people from the Zionist Hashomer Hatzair organization were waiting for me. After I left, my parents did not reply to my letters for a time. Later, my mother began writing, but no one else.'

Shalom Cholawski is Ida Milewicz's husband. They met after the war, when no one was waiting for Ida to come back to Poznań. Shalom emigrated first. He waited for her in Israel for several months. When she arrived, they lived on a kibbutz. Now they proudly show me around their place. Shalom leads me into his study, which is filled with books and manuscripts. He points out his life's work, and says, 'Only five Jews from Nieśwież survived the Holocaust. We meet once a year.' Shalom has already written 120 pages in Yiddish about Nieśwież. What am I saying? Not about Nieśwież – those 120 pages deal only with his family home and the streets where he played as a child, and about the raspberries belonging to the Sergeant-Major who lived nearby. Shalom travelled to Nieśwież in the early 1990s. He had no trouble finding his way around. He recognized every stone. He met the Sergeant-Major's son and asked him, 'Do the raspberries still grow there?' The Sergeant-Major's son replied, 'They still grow there.'

I phoned Ida Milewicz from Noach Lasman's apartment. 'Mrs Milewicz,' I said, 'I'm visiting Beniamin Anolik at the Ghetto Heroes' Kibbutz tomorrow. I'd also like to drop in on you.' From the other end of the line, I heard a young girl's voice: 'We'll be waiting for you.' The bus ride from Haifa went slowly. I finally got off at the bus stop in Ramat Hashofet. Ida and Szalom rose from the bench they were sitting on. Again, I heard that young girl's voice. 'What a magical voice,' I thought as we walked along the tree-lined kibbutz paths. We stood before a one-storey house and then sat down at the table on the porch. There was no need to hurry, as I would be staying overnight. Ida took out photo albums. She showed me books about Poznań, Chopin and Paderewski. I felt as if we were slowly slipping from that Israeli sunshine back to the street where the Milewicz family once lived. The church spire on St Wojciech's Hill came into view. Ida was standing in front of the family home. She said, 'We lived on the second floor. Frąckowiak's beer hall was downstairs.'

Ida's parents made their way from Grajewo to Poznań. Her mother Wela, whose maiden name was Kalinowska, had a brother living on Dabrowskiego Street. He said to her, 'Let your husband learn to make sausage in Białystok. When he knows how, let him come to Poznań.' Mosze Milewicz heeded his brother-in-law's advice. On arrival in Poznań, he started a wholesale meat-packing business under the supervision of the rabbinate. Their first apartment was at 5 Grobla Street, but they later moved to 7 Św. Wojciecha Street. The meat-packer's was on Masztalarska Street.

Ida was the Milewicz's eldest child. Her sisters were named Ania, Hela and Sonia. Her brothers were Izio and Wladek, whom everyone called Bobuś. Something very unfortunate befell Sonia one day, when they were living on Grobla Street. The maid took little Sonia for a walk along the River Warta. They were playing a game in which Sonia sat in a wagon, which the maid pushed energetically and then chased, but the wagon tipped over and the maid brought Sonia home crying. The little girl never got better. Nothing helped. Ida used to bring her pastries from a nearby bakery. One night, Ida went to bed and dreamt of her ailing sister. She recalls, 'I dreamt that Sonia was calling me. I got up. That was when they told me that Sonia had died. And that she had called out my name before dying.'

Grandmother Kalinowska from Grajewo was called Golda.

The Kalinowskis were wealthy Jews who traded in horses. They went deep into Russia to buy horses. Grandmother wore a wig. She made delicious things to eat, like diced herring with vinegar and sugar. On the day her grandfather died, her father travelled to his grave. On his way back, he brought Grandmother to Poznań for three months. Mama also brought her sister to live with them, along with the sister's husband and child. (Sadly, the child drowned.) The sister's husband knew no trade – all he did was pray. There was no place in Poznań for people like him. In Grajewo, he was in a different world: the synagogue, the cemetery, the Jewish tailors and the Jewish shopkeepers. There, he was among his own kind, because practically half the residents of Grajewo were Jewish.

'Hashomer Hatzair was the cradle of our youth,' recalls Ida Milewicz. 'We liked the scout uniforms and the well-trained instructors who talked about Palestine and the history of the Jews, and taught the Hebrew language and scout lore. I liked the Hachshara in preparation for life in Palestine. At the Jewish school, they looked askance at what we were doing. Mrs Propst, the principal, could not accept Zionist ideas. She would weep as she read Mickiewicz. That struck us as laughable, and it was only later that I understood what a great patriot she was.

I remember the boys from Hashomer very well. I remember Felek Mornel, who came from a wealthy family – I believe they owned a lumberyard. Felek had a lovely voice. He played and sang well. To march with Felek through the streets of Poznań was an honour. There were other boys, too: Zali Sieradzki, Mietek Krakowski (whom we called 'Quick') and Izio Sonnabend, who was a legendary figure for us. I met him years later in Australia, when Shalom was invited there to give a series of lectures. I sat with Izio in the front row. He listened to what Shalom was saying with tears in his eyes. And I sat there beside him thinking, 'The unforgettable Izio still has a sensitive spirit and heart.'

There was also Jakow Lisek, a maverick, who was our leader. He was a brilliant boy. An intellectual, he had a talent for speaking and the gift of persuasion. I met him in

Samarkand during the war. Those were very hard times for me. And the meeting itself seemed as if it had been set up. A little thief followed me around Samarkand: a homeless boy who stole in order to survive. (There were a great many of his kind.) Lonia woke me up in the morning and asked, "Where's your suitcase?" I looked around and it was gone. I began crying. I went to the police. I told them that someone had robbed me. Suddenly, Jakow Lisek appeared at my side. I froze. "Jakow," I asked, "what are you doing here?" It was incredible. To think that we would meet in Samarkand, at the police station. But Lisek had changed – he was no longer the well-groomed boy from Poznań. He was sloppy, he didn't wash or shave, and he walked around with no shoelaces in his shoes. He died soon afterwards.

I had a friend in the organization named Edzia Szlechtarz. Her family came from Wilejka. She was a hunchbacked girl who lived in Małe Garbany Street. The interesting thing is that Edzia survived, despite her appearance. She reached Israel and lived at the Evron kibbutz near Nahariya. I remember that she paid no attention at all to her deformity – she could sing and dance beautifully, and she had great joy from life. Wherever hunchbacked Edzia went, there was always a good atmosphere.

The Hashomer "nest" was a second home for us. We rebelled, ran away, broke the established norms and customs of our homes. In our scouts' meeting room, with its linoleum floor, we danced and sang. In all of it, there was so much innocence, *naïveté*, and freshness.'

When the war broke out in 1939, Ida wanted to get from Grodno to Vilnius. She was arrested crossing the border and sent to a labour camp where she worked four hours on and four hours off, around the clock. When you are under arrest, you dream of suddenly seeing a beloved face: your father, your mother, your brother. One day, a girl she had never seen before walked in and stood there helplessly. 'I invited her into my room. It turned out that she was from Białystok. She had been living in Paris, and had come back to Poland for the summer vacation. She did not manage to get out before the war started. Her name was Riwka Blinder. They did not allow us to work together, so when she went to work, she brought me her sheepskin coat, so that I could warm up in it for four hours.'

When the German–Russian war broke out, the Russians released all the Poles, including Ida, from the Gulag. She made her way to Samarkand. Then, in 1946, she was repatriated to Poland. She went to Wrocław and worked in the Solidarity Cooperative, but she could not locate any of her relatives. Someone told her that her sister Hela and brother Bobuś had escaped from Cracow and gone to hide in the woods. They were killed there, and the murderers were not Germans. Her parents had probably died in Treblinka. At work at the cooperative, someone showed her a newspaper advertisement which read: 'My name is Halina Milewicz. I am seriously ill and need help.' Ida thought it might be her sister, so she wrote to the address in the newspaper. There was no response, however. Bronek Bergman had met her brother Izydor on 'the Aryan side' in 1942, just before the notorious 'Hotel Polski' Nazi entrapment operation. Some Jews were deceived into coming out of hiding after hearing promises that they would be allowed to go abroad in exchange for German prisoners of war. They were made to pay large amounts of money to obtain passports. Izydor was supposedly one of those who went to the Hotel Polski to apply – as did Icchak Kacenelson and his son, and many, many other Jews as well.

Ida escaped from Poland in 1950. On the train ride to Szczecin she stopped off in Poznań. She sat on a bench in the waiting room, pretending to be asleep. She thought her heart would break.

Many years passed and the day came when she decided to journey to Poland. She went to Treblinka. 'It must have been here,' she thought, silently pronouncing the names of her mother and father. She travelled to Poznań and found herself in front of 7 Św. Wojciecha Street. That was her apartment, that was where Felek Mornel and the Kirszenblum family lived. Bobuś used to spend a few hours a day at Renia and Niusia Kirszenblum's, because their mother offered child-care as a part-time occupation. Ida went to Żydowska Street and stood in front of the old people's home. She took a picture of the window of Rabbi Sender's apartment. Then she took another look at the old people's home: there, on the second floor, she often sang and danced for those lonely people. She took a few steps and stopped. Adam Lewkowicz lived some-where nearby. She remembered that the door to his building had been old and neglected; now it was new. 'That is where Bronek Nergman, a friend of my brother Izi, lived. And Nojuś [Noach] Lasman, who is now in Israel writing such beautiful books, lived somewhere here.'

She says: 'I went along Wielka Street looking for the hat shop that belonged to the Postawski family. I also looked for the restaurant that Mania Moskowicz's parents ran. When her father wasn't around, we went there to drink tea with her. We would sit at the tables like street urchins. The restaurant was on the second floor. Commercial travellers ate there. I went back to Stawna Street. The Jewish Community offices and Mrs Propst's school were in that red-brick building. That is also where the Sonnabends lived. There was not a boy or girl in town who did not know the names of the Sonnabend chil-dren. There was Izi, and Nani, Adi, Rafi, Rozi, Zejmi and Naftali. I can remember the smell of the potatoes that Adi loved to fry up when he got home too late for supper. I walked along the Old Town Square. I looked for Adaś Sędziejewski's apartment and his parents' carpet store. I thought about the parents of Henia and Maks Auerbach. They had a wholesale place selling bicycle and car parts on Wielka Street, and their partners were the parents of Lola and Leosia Gerson.'

'Let's go back to the last days of August 1939,' says Ida. 'The vacation was over and I had just returned home. "Now it's time for me to do what I want to do," I told my parents. "I'm going to Grodno." Bobuś did not want to let me go. He ran out on to the pavement after me (the maid was with him), scream-ing, "Ida, take me with you!" As if he knew that I was head-ing for a better world. That I would survive.'

160

23 'Who are you, Mr Lasman?'

On 11 December 1939 the Gestapo forced the Jewish community to organize an assembly of all the Jews living in Poznań They were supposed to turn out at 8 o'clock the next morning 'in the Główna district'. Those who showed up were placed in a barrack marked by a sign reading 'Für Isaak, für Sara'. They were robbed of their personal effects. Each of them was allowed to keep 50 zloty. Press photographers took pictures that day of people in the camp who had Semitic features. They were ordered to pose for those pictures. Two days later, the Germans loaded them all into cattle-trucks. Thus began the exodus of the Jews of Poznań, only a few of whom survived. Noach Lasman is one of them.

'Who are you, Mr Lasman?' I ask. The question is addressed more to myself than to the elderly gentleman who is seated across from me and watching me carefully. I have been in the Lasmans' Jerusalem apartment for several hours, and I already know a great deal because Noach has been writing his memoirs for years. He has a good memory and can reel off details, dates and names. His wife Clila serves us delicacies as we sip coffee and tea. I sense that there is pain and despair concealed somewhere behind those systematic narratives. Perhaps Tauba and Abram, his parents, come to him in dreams. Perhaps they speak to him: 'Dear son.' And he repays them the debt of memory. He knows that every time he writes down a name it is like a pebble on a gravestone, and will never again be lost.

Noach is aware of what happened in Poznań because he was told things by people he met later. In the meantime, he and the other deportees rode in the cattle-trucks. Most of them were sent to eastern Poland, not far from the Russian border. The people from Poznań were resettled in Brzeźnica. Several of the men set off on foot for Ostrów Lubelski, some ten kilometres away. It was cold – 40 degrees below zero. Fortunately, the local Jews sent a horse-drawn cart and food after them, and helped them to reach the town. Most of them were quartered in the synagogue or the mikvah, and others were placed with families.

Ostrów Lubelski was a poor small town on the edge of the Lublin forests. It had a population of 4,000, of whom 30 per cent were Jewish. There were sandy roads leading to Lubartowo and Parczewo. Those who fled to Russia, however, did not follow those roads. There were others who left for Warsaw or other cities. In Israel, Noach Lasman found a *Sefer Izkor* (a memorial book) containing photocopies of documents associated with Ostrów. There are names there like Kobliner, Kempinski and Szlamowicz. In mid 1941, Kobliner received a 'boat ticket' to Santo Domingo from a brother in the United States. Unfortunately, the ticket had to be collected person in Hamburg.

'In Ostrów,' says Noach, 'there were not only Jews from Poznań but also refugees from Bohemia and Austria.' In May 1942 there were over 3,000 Jews there. The local people treated them well. The men worked for the German army, or at draining the marshes. There were powerful leftist and Russian partisan units in the local forests and marshes. In those same forests and marshes, a local man named Chil Grynszpan commanded the largest Jewish partisan band in the general government. In the summer of 1942 his unit numbered over 120 people. The partisans watched over a 'family camp' where another 200 people were concealed. One of them was Rózia Zalc of Poznań, whom Noach met in Łódź after the war.

In November 1942 the Jews had to leave Ostrów on foot. They were marched to Lubartów. Three days later, all of them – including the people from Poznań – were sent from there in a transport to the death camp at Bełżec.

Let us return to Poznań in 1939. The war had just begun. Noach's parents escaped from the city and reached Koniń. But feeling that their flight was useless, they returned home. Several days later, the Germans entered Poznań. Since the son-in-law of the owner of their building liked the look of their apartment, the Lasmans were evicted. That son-in-law had just signed the *Volksliste*. Noach returned to Poznań from his summer camp in early October to find that the city already had a German look to it. Poles and the first Jews were being shot at Fort VII. Dawid Galanternik of Kórnik was among them. Noach knew him quite well. Before the war, Galanternik had named his dog 'Little Hitler'. Noach remembers that the Germans took over Dobski's sweet shop. They translated the sign reading 'Dogs and Jews Not Allowed' into German, adding the phrase *'und Polen'* for good measure. The Germans began arresting Poles. They took them to the Główna Street camp, which was next to the station, and from there they were all sent east. The Jews assumed that the same fate awaited them. Their shops had already been confiscated, the synagogues closed and the Jewish library liquidated.

Noach's parents knew that they had to get out before they ended up on Główna Street. But where could they go? And to whom? They had relatives in Kórnik, Kalisz and Konin, but those places were not worth even considering. Someone mentioned Łosice. Shortly before the war, one of Noach's uncles had embarked on married life there with a girl from a *shtetl* in the Siedlce region, near the border with Russia. They decide to make a move. 'We were in Łosice a few days later,' Noach Lasman recalls. The journey came off without a hitch because someone had provided Abram Lasman with a *Bescheinigung* that allowed him to travel with all his baggage. That cursed baggage! Noach often thinks that, if they had only lost that baggage along the way, they might have made it to Russia, and all of them might have been saved.

They reached the town. Some 40 people from Poznań were in Łosice during the war: Abram and Tauba Lasman with their children Noach, Moniek and Nadzia; Noach's uncles, Icek and Szmul; the Mordkowicz, Szwarcbard, Lewin and Moszkowicz families; Ojnik and Fryda Aron. The Borensztajns and Lodzia Sędziejewska lived in the nearby town of Mordy, and the Hamburgers in Sokołów Podlaskie. Noach corresponded with Kuba Globus and Lutek Rajn, who were in Koniń. He sent letters to Lucynka Abramowicz in the Warsaw ghetto.

The Jews in Podlasia were murdered in late 1942. None of them went to camps. Beginning in December 1942, Jews were killed on the spot wherever they were found. The bounty for a Jew, dead or alive, was a litre of vodka, two litres of petrol and five kilos of sugar.

'Who survived, Mr Lasman?'
'Hana and Chaim Mordkowicz survived.
Their sons, Zalus and Borys.
Fimek Borensztajn.
And me.'

'Let's go back to the prewar days in Poznań. Many of my friends in primary school belonged to Hashomer Hatzair,' Noach Lasman recalls. 'For one reason or another, I did not sign up. Perhaps it was the discipline that put me off. In secondary school, I found myself in a new atmosphere that was hostile and anti-Semitic. I felt lonely, so I founded a sports club with some other boys – Kuba Globus and Józek Haftel were the leaders. We met on Fridays on ground near the station. The ground was part of Józek Haftel's father's lumberyard. Romek Rozenband, Jurek Janowski, Olek Pszenica, Józek Bros, Lutek Leder and Tusiek Hirszhorn went there. We played volleyball and ran. We saved up money and bought a discus, javelin and a shot. We also prepared topics and held discussions in Józek's father's office. We talked about Palestine, about forthcoming holidays, and Jewish life in Poland and around the world.

We were not an elite group in any way. We kept in touch with our friends in Hashomer Hatzair. We were the same age as the Banir troop and we had friends among them. Their leaders were Zaluś Mordkowicz and Anna Milewicz. They tried to recruit the members of our group. Zaluś started nego-tiating with me. We knew each other well and I spent a lot of time in his home. His brother Szmulek was my best friend. Zaluś attended the Machine Construction Engineering School. He was well-read and worldly. We had our reserva-tions, but Zaluś proved to us that the life of the Jews should change in our generation and that we should return to agri-cultural work. He said, "The Jewish proletariat and the Jewish farmer will not be backward. They will earn a living and be intellectuals at the same time." He impressed us, but our sense of honour made us hold back at first.

In the meantime, we were reading in the newspapers about what Hitler was saying and doing. At the same time, the right-wing parties in Poland were demanding the expulsion of Jews from public life. We also encountered anti-Semitism at the Berger secondary school. Our classmates and teachers stressed their negative attitude towards Jews. "They are para-sites living at the cost of the Poles," they said. The *numerus clausus* and *numerus nullus* were introduced at the universi-ties. We realized that we would have to emigrate. The Hashomer ideology would permit us to leave Poland with our heads held high and to build a new society. That was impor-tant – to leave with honour, rather than running away.

Then came the autumn of 1938. The Germans drove thou-sands of Jews holding Polish passports to Zbąszyń. The Poznań Jewish community joined in the aid action. Students taking part were given time off by the school. Senior members of Hashomer went to Zbąszyń to help set up a transit camp. Some of the refugees came to Poznań. Jewish Community officials found families for them to stay with. Within a few days most of them had found places for themselves in various parts of Poland. None of us felt that we would be in the same situation a year later. It was that wave of refugees that led us to join Hashomer Hatzair without reservation.

We boys talked about other things besides politics in our group. I can remember discussions where, even as we blushed, we argued about the right to free love or trial mar-riages. It was comical, childish and beautiful. After all, the majority of us had never even kissed a girl. In fact, we were very puritanical. If someone had a girlfriend, the case was discussed at a meeting. We went away for a winter camp in late December 1938. We were officially inducted into the organization at Lag Ba'Omer. In the summer the whole group went to the village of Wielki Dęby on the Vistula for three weeks. That was near Dobrzyń. It was August, and we were all talking about mobilization. And then, one afternoon, the police came and ordered us to pack up and cross by boat to Dobrzyń. From there, we travelled to Włocławek, where we found a wartime atmosphere. I returned to Poznań in October 1939 to find that most of my friends were gone. I learned from Zejmi that our banner had been packed in a metal case and buried in Szeląg.'

Aside from memories, I have a group photograph of the Banir organization. It was taken on an excursion to Kobylepole. Borys Mordkowicz and Bronek Bergman are missing, since they were students at the secondary school in Kalisz. But the photograph shows Tadek Cyruliczak, Zuzia Kutner, Zejmi Sonnabend, Nojuś Lasman – that's me – Romek Rozenband, Danek Vogelnest, Józek Lisek, Zaluś Mordkowicz, Moniek Lasman, Kuba Globus, Józek Haftel, Tusiek Hirszhorn, Adam Redlich, Lutek Leder, Bronka Ickowicz, Felek Lachman, Bela Sędziejewska, Inka Rowińska, Hela Milewicz, Lucyna Abramowicz, Dorka Aszner, Kranka Lisner, Truda Lewin and Anna Milewicz. Of the people in that photograph, the ones who survived are Bela Sędziejewska, Romek Rozenband, and me.'

'Let's go back to Łosice,' said Noach. 'My parents wrote to the Mordkowiczes, who had travelled to Warsaw after being deported to Ostrów Lubelski. "Come join us here and we can sit out the war." The Mordkowiczes arrived along with their sons Zaluś, Szmulek and Borys. We lived mostly by selling things. We did forced labour, for which no one paid us. A ghetto was set up on 1 December 1941. The price of food rose and hunger became more and more acute. In the spring of 1942 the Germans sent some of the young people to the labour camp in Siedlce. Zaluś and I went on the same transport. We stuck together in camp. On 22 August the Germans carried out an 'operation' throughout the region, in which approximately 30,000 Jews were murdered or deported. The Mordkowiczes went into hiding, and they were later put in what was left of the Łosice ghetto. Their son Borys was killed immediately after the operation.

My family died during that operation. My mother Tauba. My father Abram. My brother Moniek and my sister Nadzia. News of the Łosice massacre reached us two weeks later. I read in a letter about the death of my family. The Mordkowiczes wrote, "Get out of there and come to us." They convinced us, and within several days we were all together. We escaped from the ghetto and were hidden in a peasant's potato cellar until liberation. One of the survivors described the murder operation in Łosice to me. I have described those events in my book *Fifty Kilometers from Treblinka*. From what that witness told me, it seems that the Jews heard gunfire at around five in the morning. They were all ordered to prepare to march. At around ten o'clock, they were to assemble on the town square. They were greeted with gunfire. "I thought it was a pogrom," the boy who had survived told me. "Some people, like Dr Zajd with his daughter Dziunia and her fiancée, even tried to escape into the side streets. But two policeman, Purath and Zieliński caught them. Zajd gave them dollars and valuables to set them free. They took the bribe and then shot them. Sick people were loaded on to horse-drawn carts, and the rest were left in a marching column. The procession was going in the direction of Siedlce. Starting on the outskirts of Łosice, they shot people from the column. I saw one woman take a little girl off to the side of the road. Just as she pulled down the little girl's panties, they were both hit by a series of machine-gun fire. We had to walk 32 kilometres in that heat. The column moved in a cloud of dust, leaving corpses behind. I realized that it was a death march."'

Noach Lasman continues: 'The Red Army set me free on 1 August. We greeted our liberators with joy. Only a handful of us Jews survived. We read the manifesto, and it seemed that Poland would not become another Soviet Republic. One thing was sure, we thought: it would be a Poland without anti-Semitism. We convinced ourselves that anti-Semitism would be impossible after the massacre of the Jewish nation. I can remember how amazed we were when we saw how an unknown hand had written "Jew", "*kike*", "servant of the Jews" and "Jewish lackey" on posters with pictures of the members of the Polish National Liberation Committee. It turned out that anti-Semitism still existed, even after the departure of the Germans and the death of the Jews. An unknown assailant threw a hand-grenade into the building where we were living, after shouting "Death to the Jews". Fortunately, no one was injured. Stones wrapped in pieces of paper with insulting messages written on them were also thrown. So, when mobilization was announced in late August, I decided to join the army. I was thinking then about my murdered family, not about the future political system in Poland. They had a farewell evening for us, with vodka and *kielbasa* (sausage). A collection was taken, and each potential avenger of Hitler received 2,500 zloty. At the end, Miller, a veteran of the rebellion in Treblinka, called us aside and gave us additional money out of his own pocket.'

Noach Lasman returned to Poznań after the war. He worked in the Central Committee of Jews while studying geography at the university. He moved in with Clila, found a job and became a father. After the events of June 1956, his boss came up to him. Filipowski said, 'I just came back from Warsaw, and at the station I saw a lot of Jews emigrating to Israel.' Noach recalls that the news came as a shock to me. I told Clila all about it, and we were too excited to sleep all night. We decided to go and see acquaintances in Wałbrzych, Wrocław and Łódź. In the end, we made up our minds: "We're leaving."'

Noach (Nojuś) Lasman wrote a letter to the Polish president in 1990. He had just returned from Poland, having visited Poznań, Treblinka, Łosice, Tykocin and Siedlce. He asked why there were no memorial plaques on the Jewish school or the prayer house in Poznań. In Łosice he had found gravestones in the courtyard of a private home. The woman who owned the house told him, 'I'll give back the gravestones on the condition that they pave my courtyard in return.' That is why

Noach Lasman wrote in his letter: 'Mr President, is there another place on this earth where the gravestones of the Jewish nation are treated as private property? Is there another place where the descendants of the deceased have no right to their gravestones?'

24 Jakub's Sign

His parents came from Prużany, a small town in Byelorussia, somewhere near Bereza Kartuska. In search of a better life after their wedding, the young Abramowiczes moved to Łódź. In 1925 they took up residence on Marcinkowskiego Avenue, across from the post office in Poznań. Jakub Abramowicz and his brother Cylke ran a wholesale business on the Old Town Square. Olek remembers that a sign reading 'Upholstery' hung over the door. It was a place where you could buy gobelins, rugs and curtains. It was a big shop, beautifully furnished, but today not a trace of it remains.

The anti-Semitic newspaper *In the Pillory* soon took note of the Abramowicz's shop. Early in 1933 (issue no. 19), the editor wrote:

> Who would have expected that, in our list of Jewish firms, we would pass over the firm at 80–82 Old Town Square, belonging to the Jew Abramowicz? Even if we did miss out on this Poznań figure, it is worth taking a look at him personally and stating that he is in tip-top shape, lives like a king, and enjoys great success. You may ask, dear reader, how he makes a living. Through cunning. After all, he sells everything he can, and namely curtains, wall-hangings, thread and linings, and of course it all reeks of cheapness.

All the Jews who settled in or returned to Poznań were greeted in similar vein. A Jewish family, the Pakulas, found themselves in Poznań in 1933. *In the Pillory* published an article entitled 'A Scandal':

> The Jewish family of the Pakulas, numbering four persons, arrived recently from Germany. Pakula, a German

subject, is a political *émigré*. Pakula's efforts at finding a place to live in Poznań were crowned with success, when he found a compliant *shabbes-goy*, namely, Dr Antoni Seg— of Dąbrowskiego Street, who accepted the family as boarders. It should be added that this occurred without the knowledge, and even against the wishes of the owner of the building.

The journalist refrained from giving the full name of Dr Seg— . He was giving him time to think things over. Further on, he attacked only the Pakula family, who had the effrontery to apply for a licence to trade in livestock. 'As if it were not enough,' the writer grumbled, 'that the Jew illegally takes advantage of Polish hospitality, he also has the gall to attempt to obtain permission to carry on trade. And all of this at a time when thousands of our Polish brothers are suffering hunger and poverty.'

At first, Olek went to the German *Freischule*. When he was ten years old, his parents transferred him to the school run by Mrs Propst. When he finished that school, he passed the entrance examination for the Paderewski *gymnazjum*, but was soon expelled from there. 'I had a history teacher who didn't like Jews,' he recalls. 'And I had a big mouth. I argued with him, so they threw me out for unruly behaviour.'

Ida Fink too recounts anti-Jewish incidents at the Paderewski school in her story 'Julia'. She changes the names of the family that moved to Poznań from a village in the eastern borderlands.

In the second year that she lived in Poznań, two things happened that violently diminished her affection for the city that she had admired for its cleanliness and order. Her older son, Dawid, was roughed up at school by classmates shouting 'Beat the Jew, Beat the Jew!' From that time on, the boy began to be hunched over, as if he were waiting always for a blow to fall. The second incident occurred in the beautiful lobby of the Philharmonic, and it was just as eloquent, although more discreet in its form. During intermission in a

171

concert by a renowned pianist, Julia heard a remark uttered *sotto voce*: 'You can't get away from them even here.' She passed up her two favourite Beethoven sonatas and left the Philharmonic Hall, never to return.

That was the year when signs were hung in many establishments reading 'Dogs and Jews Not Allowed'. All that remained was strolling along the banks of the river that ran through that clean, Germanized city. Her sons breathed a sigh of relief when the school year ended in June and their mother began packing their bags for vacation. They were to spend it in their home-town of Z.

After his expulsion Olek could not even dream of being accepted at another secondary school in Poznań. It was there-fore decided to send him to Równe, where his mother's sister lived. That is how Olek began attending a private Jewish school, 800 kilometres from Poznań. He only came home twice a year. He was in Poznań when the war broke out, while his sister Ester, a university student, was in Warsaw. In September his father sent Olek and his mother to stay with relatives in Pruzhany. When he got there, he had nothing but the clothes he was wearing – he had not been allowed to take anything with him. The Russians soon entered Prużany. Olek continued going to school, but now it was a Russian school. He took military training and became an instructor. Thanks to this promotion, the Russians did not shave Olek's head, as they did with the other boys. As soon as he passed his final school examinations, the Germans entered Prużhany. They arrested all men with shaven heads, on the assumption that they were soldiers. Olek went free because he still had some hair on his head.

Towards the end of 1941 a ghetto was set up for the Jews, and Olek and his mother lived there for nearly two years. After the liquidation of the ghetto in the summer of 1943 they found themselves in a cattle-truck heading for Treblinka. 'I tore out a board and jumped out when the train was going around a curve,' he says. 'I injured my arm and leg.' The curve was important, because that was the only time that it was possible to escape by jumping. This happened at night, near Mińsk Mazowiecki. Olek removed his yellow badge and set off for Warsaw on foot. Since he spoke German well, he registered at a recruiting office as a volunteer for labour in Germany. They quartered him in a dormitory at the University of Warsaw. When a typhus epidemic broke out, they began shaving all the hair off everyone's body. 'I was afraid that they would see that I was a Jew,' he says. So he escaped from the camp and went into hiding in Warsaw.

He spent the first day riding trams. Night fell, and he had to get off. He found a place to sleep in some ruins near the tram barn. Through the small window in the cellar, he could see a sign reading '35 Radzymińska Street'. For several days he ate four candies per day and smoked two cigarettes. He had no money to buy more. He was afraid in Warsaw: 'Anyone who walked the streets unwashed and badly dressed had to be a Jew in hiding. People like that were caught by the police, or sometimes by Poles, and turned over to the Germans.'

He repeated to himself, 'I'm not going to die,' and thought of the knife he carried in one of his high boots. Extortionists caught him once and shoved him into a doorway. Out of the corner of his eye, he noticed a board. He grabbed it and lashed out blindly at his attackers. 'I have to get out of here,' he said after this incident. He sold his jacket, bought a half a loaf of bread, and set out for Częstochowa. Once again, he went to a recruiting office. 'I want to go to Germany to work,' he told the official, although he realized that the only people who went to such places were those with something to escape from. The clerk asked him, 'What's your name?' Olek Abramowicz says, 'And I saw that sign from Warsaw before my eyes, so I told him, "Aleksander Radzymiński".'

They sent him to Katowice. He worked repairing railroad semaphore signals. Later, he ended up in a factory in Piekary. The front lines were approaching. Olek remembered that he was a Russian soldier. People like that who were caught behind the German lines were shot. Fortunately, his name was not Abramowicz, but Radzymiński. He travelled to Lublin and joined the army there. He made it to Gdynia by the time the war ended, and stayed in Jelitkowa, where he was put in charge of the fisheries.

There was a boy from Poznań in the same company. His sister came to visit him in Gdańsk one day. She was about to get married and was searching for bedding, pillows and clothing. They helped her, since there were abandoned German homes everywhere. Olek told her that he lived at 28 Marcinkowski Street. When the girl got back to Poznań, she went to that address to ask about the Radzymiński family from the second floor. 'That's where the Abramowiczes lived,' said the building superintendent, explaining that from among the whole family, only Jakub had returned – without his wife and children. 'The woman was not stupid,' says Olek after all these years. She wrote him a letter with a postscript reading, 'Greetings from Mr Abramowicz.' Olek immediately requested leave and travelled to Poznań. 'I went to see the superintendent. He told me, "Abramowicz was here, but he won't be coming back until tomorrow." So I went to see that girl. My father was at her place. I told him about mother, and asked about my sister. "Ester survived," my father said. "She's living in Łódź. And Lucynka with the beautiful braids, your brother Cylke's daughter? She died in the Warsaw ghetto."'

Olek stayed in Poznań with his father. In fact, he stayed there by himself, because his father died before the end of 1945. Olek went to Wrocław to requisition some former German property. He found sewing machines and delivered them to Kalisz and Poznań. During one of these expeditions, he met Jurek Janowski in the ruins of Wrocław. They drank vodka together that evening, because otherwise it would have been difficult to talk about what they had been through. Olek made an illegal crossing of the Polish–German border in 1946. He got to the American zone and was soon smuggled out to Palestine. He lived in Holon, a city founded on the bare sands in 1935. He felt good, because there were many textile workers from Łódź there. When his sister Ester moved from a kibbutz to Tel Aviv, she was nearby. Olek travels a great deal. Whether he goes to Alaska or Kenya, he always brings home a new knife. He has a modest collection of them. The one he is missing is the knife that he carried in his boot while hiding in Warsaw.

Olek visited Poznań in 1989. He went to the Hotel Bazar on Marcinkowski Street and handed his passport to the receptionist.

'Why do you want to stay here?' the young man asked him. 'There are so many modern hotels in Poznań.'

'Because I used to live on this street,' he answered. 'I played here with my friends. I walked past here on my way to meet my father at Hirschlik's restaurant.'

He walked out of the hotel onto the Old Town Square. However, he could not find the building where there used to be a sign reading 'Upholstery'. Nor could he find his father's grave, or the family records at city hall. So he went to the building where he lived before the war. He peeked in through the window, and then studied the list of residents. He saw that there were three families living in their old apartment. He did not knock at the door. He was afraid that someone might ask, 'What does a Jew from Israel want here?'

25 Lettuce with Sour Cream

He has a warm, friendly voice. What a shame, I think, that we have only a few minutes to talk. I know that there will be too little time for him to tell me about his childhood in Poznań and about the Łódź ghetto, or about his wanderings in Russia, his return to Poland and his life in Israel. Yet the meeting takes place, and Adek Redlich takes me for a tour of his life.

We are soon at Małe Garbany Street, in front of the building with the number 7 on it, where he lived with his parents Gustawa and Pinkus. We make our way to the Jewish school, to his classroom and his friends from the school benches: Jurek Janowski and Bronek Bergman. Adek talks about his father, who was a representative for an Austrian bank that had its headquarters on Floriańska Street in Cracow. About how he tried to get into the commercial and Berger secondary schools, but failed because there were limits on Jewish admissions. So he had to travel to the school in Oborniki. He did not regret this, since Mr Fogl was such an outstanding principal. 'I was walking down Allenby Street in Tel Aviv one day,' Redlich recalls, 'when I heard a voice saying, "You're from Poznań." I stood there dumbfounded. I could not believe my own eyes. Standing there before me was Mrs Kwaśniewska, a history teacher from Oborniki. It turned out that she lived in England and had come to Israel on a package tour.'

Adek's father, Pinkus Redlich, was mobilized before the start of the war. Along with the rest of the Poznań Army, he was taken prisoner, but managed to escape. He went to his hometown of Łódź rather than to Poznań, where it would have been too easy to fall into the hands of the German police. He arranged to wait in Łódź for his wife and son. 'We travelled there by train. Unfortunately, the train was bombed somewhere between Września and Strzałków. We set out for Łódź on foot. By the time we were reunited with my father, we had to put on the yellow patch.'

One day – Adek remembers the moment precisely – he was walking between his parents when they encountered a German patrol. An SS man called him over, and then struck him so hard that it broke his nose. Adek told his parents, 'We have to get out of the ghetto.' They reached Białystok by way of Małkinia, wandering through Russia all the way from the Ukraine to Georgia.

When the war ended they returned to Poland, unaware of the scale of the tragedy that had occurred. Adek lived in Wałbrzych. His parents went to Germany because his father had held German citizenship before the war. They lived there only for a short while before his father was killed when he stepped in front of a car while crossing the street.

In 1950 the young Redlichs applied for the first time for permission to emigrate to Israel. They received the required papers, but these were withdrawn by the secret police at the last moment. In the meantime, their baggage was already in Italy and somebody else had already moved into their apartment. Fortunately, their neighbours helped out. It was not until 1957 that the Redlichs, who by now had two children, applied again for permission to emigrate. This time they were permitted to leave Poland.

More than 40 years later, Adek Redlich revisited the country of his birth. He took his sons along, rented a car, and drove them around to the 'most important' places. Their last stop was in Poznań, where he treated them to lettuce with sour cream.

26 Metaphysics at Dawn

Professor Bauman was born in Poznań and had lived in an apartment building on Prus Street. I asked him if he'd like me to send him some photographs of the building. He said he would, as he had not been in Poznań for almost 30 years.

We were talking in a small room at the Jewish Historical Institute on a gloomy March day. I was asking questions and the professor was answering them without putting his pipe down. Poznań soon faded into the background and we talked about his book *Modernity and the Holocaust*. Next door, in the 'silver skyscraper' on Tłomacka Street, a scholarly conference was underway on the fiftieth anniversary of the Warsaw Ghetto Uprising. The professor was a participant and, like everyone, he posed the question, 'How could it have happened?'

'I spent my childhood in Poznań,' said Zygmunt Bauman. 'The apartment buildings on Prus Street, Jeżycki Square and Słowacki and Kraszewski Streets were my whole world. I can recall going to the countryside on vacation only once as a child. My sister and I also made excursions to the Botanical Gardens, on the far side of which there were fields of corn-flowers and poppies in those days. I cannot recall anti-Semitism from my primary school years. Of course, I had my enemies – boys from Jeżycki Square. They used to rough me up, but I don't think that was connected with my background. It was probably my belly that provoked them. I was a fat boy then. I grew up in the kitchen and my mother, a good cook, was always giving me something to eat. That is how things stayed until 1938, when I passed the entrance examination for the Berger *Gymnazjum*.'

The Berger *Gymnazjum* was the only secondary school in Poznań where Jews were subject only to a *numerus clausus*, and not a *numerus nullus*. Zygmunt Bauman continued: 'Apart from me, there were four other Jewish boys in the ghetto benches. Unofficially, I was also friends with other boys. One of them, Hryniewicz, became a physician after the war. The interesting thing is that I cannot remember the names of my teachers, only their nicknames. My favourite was "Tomato", a splendid Polish teacher. He had a big red nose. When he opened the classroom door, the first thing that came into sight was that red nose, followed some time later by the rest of the teacher. I am sure that some sort of closer bond with the teachers would have formed if I had been at the school longer. But there wasn't time. I only finished one year before the war broke out.'

The Baumans were a poor Jewish family. The father, Maurycy, had a shop on Koniecka Street. He went bankrupt during the depression and spent many months in a fruitless search for work. From those years Zygmunt Bauman recalls a violent knocking at the door. He was six years old. The door opened abruptly and his father was carried in on a stretcher. The orderlies said, 'He tried to commit suicide.' He tried to drown himself by jumping into the River Warta. Scouts saved him. The whole affair was blown up when it hit the local newspapers, but the furore probably helped him to find a job soon afterwards. He became a bookkeeper.

'My father was a very capable man, but my grandfather neglected his education,' Zygmunt Bauman recalls. He remembers how his father would sit reading into the night. He taught himself several languages this way, but it was passive knowledge, since he could not speak those languages. In sum, he had an unfulfilled life. As a bookkeeper, he worked for avaricious people with small-town imaginations, among whom there was no place for him to realize his dreams and ambitions.

The family went to the synagogue on Stawna Street once a year, at Yom Kippur – the only day that his father fasted. But his grandfather was an Orthodox Jew, the kind you saw on

179

the streets of the Polish *shtetl*. 'I was terrified of him,' Zygmunt Bauman recalls. 'He wanted to force me to study the Bible. We did not get along because his world struck me as very distant and alien. At the time, I was a voracious reader of completely different books: the novels of Makuszyński, Kraszewski, May and Cooper. There was no place for the religious reading of my *shtetl* grandfather.

When war broke out the Baumans fled from Poznań staying first with relatives of Zygmunt's mother in Włocławek and then, soon afterwards crossing the border into Russia. They were resettled in Vakhtan, in the Kirov *oblast* (district). It was a settlement lost in the forest, populated by lumberjacks.

'There was terrible hunger there,' Zygmunt Bauman recalls. One day his parents left him at home because he had abscesses on his legs. His mother worked in the fields and his father went to seek employment in a nearby settlement. He remembers that his mother would leave behind two bowls of soup: one for her son and one for her husband. The 15-year-old Zygmunt ate his own portion first. Later, he looked out the window, waiting for his father to arrive. He could not wait. He was still hungry. He thought, 'He's bound to stay overnight with acquaintances,' so he ate his father's portion. Yet his father returned – to find an empty bowl! 'This has pained my conscience terribly ever since,' says Bauman.

When he was hardly more than a boy, he was drafted into the Moscow militia. Three months later he was in the 6th Light Artillery Battalion of the 4th Infantry Division. He was wounded in the battle of Kołobrzeg. After the war, he was drafted along with the rest of the 4th Division into the Internal Security Corps, where he instructed propaganda officers on how they should talk to the soldiers. He finished his studies, writing a master's thesis with Julian Hochfeld. However, he was discharged from the army because of his father's contacts with the Israeli embassy. Maurycy Bauman had gone to the embassy to ask about his chances of emigrating from Poland. His son, already a major (retired), remained an ardent communist.

In October 1956 Zygmunt Bauman believed the things that Władysław Gomułka said. However, he grew more sceptical. He began researching Western sociology. By the 1960s he was reading the structuralists more often than Marx. In 1967 he opened the Polish People's Anthropology Laboratory under the aegis of the Warsaw University Chair of Sociology. At that point, the secret police began taking an interest in him. On 6 January 1968 he turned in his party membership card, and in March he took the side of the students. On 25 March he was dismissed from the university (along with Maria Hirszowicz, Leszek Kołakowski, Bronisłw Baczka, Włodzimierz Brus and Stefan Morawski). In June the Baumans and their daughters left for Israel. Customs officers confiscated their suitcases at the Gdańsk Station in Warsaw. 'To this day I can remember what was in those suitcases,' says his wife, Janina Bauman. 'They contained manuscripts of books my husband had not yet published, school notebooks belonging to my daughters, photographs, keepsakes, and my own manuscripts that had survived the war.'

Three years later, they moved from Israel to England. They said that they were fleeing from yet another variety of nationalism. Not until 1988 did they receive permission to visit Poland, and it was later still, in 1994, that they came to Poznań.

Zygmunt Bauman is professor of sociology at the University of Leeds. His books are finally being published in Poland. Crowds of interested observers attend his seminars here. He demands acceptance of the fact that other people have different views, appeals for human solidarity, and talks about the postmodern world.

In 1981 Janina Bauman accidentally came across fragments of her wartime manuscript, written when she was in the ghetto and while hiding on the Aryan side. 'At first, they survived by some miracle in a building that I left at the time of the Warsaw Uprising,' she recalls. 'When I returned there nine months later, the ruins were still standing just as they had been. I looked for the manuscript, which I had hidden under a leg of the piano. I found it and concealed it in a drawer. My mother took it to Israel in 1957, when she went to join my sister. She had a great attachment to my writing. What I had written while hiding became a part of her. She copied some of my memoirs by hand. My mother died, and later on my sister also. I realized that I was the last one who remembered. I told myself: "You have to write it down." Then the memories flowed in my direction unbidden. I wrote as if I were taking dictation. I felt as if I was again that 14-year-old girl from the ghetto. I recalled not only incidents and names, but also melodies and smells. I remembered that it was in the ghetto that I became aware of my Jewishness. That is where my feeling of community with the Jews was born. It was the ghetto that taught me that the meaning of Jewishness is a shared fate. Nothing more.'

Professor Bauman likes to talk about the first metaphysical experience in his life: what he calls 'the unusual early morning' several years ago when he left his hotel to walk to the Old Town Square in Poznań. Suddenly, after I had taken a few steps, my whole past came back to me. I felt like someone who had never left Poznań. From that moment, I knew the name of every street. I was on Paderewski Street when someone came up to me and asked me how to get to Marcinkowski Street. "Just up there and turn left," I replied, without a moment's hesitation.'

27 Jewish Cabbage Soup

The car is standing at an intersection in Jerusalem. We are waiting for the light to turn. Viola Wein lights a cigarette. She is talking on the telephone, arranging a hundred things at once, and I have no idea how she manages to hear my questions – about where she was born, about the scene at the Gdańsk Station in Warsaw, about the Jewish stigma in Poland and the Polish stigma in Israel.

'The atmosphere was tense and hysterical. At the Gdańsk Station, where *that train* left for Vienna, I ran into people whom I had never thought of as Jewish. I met a student of mine from Koło. He tried to convince me that he was only going as far as Vienna and that he had been placed in *that car* by accident. When the train began moving, I stood looking out of the window. As I felt the earth slipping away from under my feet, he came up to me and said, "I am a Jew. I only found out a couple of weeks ago, when they were shouting 'Zionists to Zion!' on the streets. That was when my parents told me who I am."

There were crowds of people on the platform. Anybody could find out what time the Chopin Express left for Vienna. It was very moving, as always, to say goodbye to friends. I saw people whom I had not seen for several years. I thought that it was a demonstration, an act of courage, for them to be there. The secret police were everywhere. it was as if those people were saying, "Let them see us here."

I remember wandering the streets of Warsaw. I lived at 5 Chopin Street. I spent the last days on the city streets. Perhaps I wanted to take along the greatest possible amount of the air from the banks of the Vistula. We were in a sort of euphoria. I would meet friends and we would go for a drink. We gave away our money, because we were only allowed to take five dollars out of Poland. And a few things. My father had an enormous library, but he had to leave most of his books in Poland. At first, they would not let us take our piano, but people from the Music Academy helped us. They stated that playing the piano was my trade, and that I would be unable to make a living without my instrument. Later it turned out that I could have bought myself a new piano for the amount of money I had to pay as customs duty.

I was too small to have memories of Poznań. I only know the city from hearing people talk about it. We lived in the basement of a three-storey apartment. From those first months of my life, I can remember the flowered blanket in which I was taken to Warsaw. I also remember our nanny – a beautiful woman who tried to commit suicide while my little brother and I were asleep in the nursery. She turned on the gas. My mother came home at the last moment. If she hadn't, we would all have been asphyxiated.

My mother gave birth to me in a hospital. When the sisters asked her what she wanted to name her little daughter, she said, "Ester". That was the name of my grandmother on the side of my grandfather, Rabbi Josef Wein of Lwów. One of the sisters told her sternly, "We're not going to register any Ester in our hospital."

Poland is landscapes, first dreams, a young girl's tears. It's the Masurian lakes, Mickiewicz, the music of Chopin. The atmosphere of the student clubs and discussions among intellectuals splitting hairs. And it's also a feeling of intellectualism more than of Jewishness. My friends were Poles first of all. Jews were in the Jewish club on Nowogrodzka Street. It was my boyfriend, a Pole, who dragged me to that club, perhaps because something impressed him, aroused his curiosity.

At home, of course, there were the holidays of Hanukkah, Yom Kippur and Purim. But in all of these there was the dualism that I wrote about in *The Mismatch*. Do you remember the cover of that book? It shows a Hanukkah candelabra out of which grows a Polish Christmas tree, and the tree is topped by a Star of David. A mismatch is when nothing fits anything else. In Israel my mother doesn't fit in. An Arab woman doesn't fit into her Jewish surroundings, a servant doesn't fit into the family. But they all exist, work and live somehow.

My friend Agnieszka M. once asked me if I could write a
text for her on my computer. I said yes. That evening, I decided to check whether the machine was working. I sat down
and began to write. That is how the short story 'Maryśka'
came into being. I was touched. I felt as if someone were giving me instructions. Agnieszka dropped in and I gave her the
story to read. Agnieszka is not one of those people who stick
their necks out. I had to wait for her opinion. She finally said,
"Viola, you must write."

Several months went by. Reporters from Polish Radio in
Warsaw came to do a programme on Spielberg. I was their
guide and interpreter. Later, I got a cassette with a recording
of the programme. For the first time, I heard myself talking
about one thing only, instead of 28 things at once. On that
programme, an actress read a fragment of one of my stories. I
was touched as I listened. Later someone said on the air that
the fragment was part of a larger work. I was flabbergasted
and phoned Alicja M. and told her, "But I'm not writing a
novel!" She said, "So write one. There are three months before
the deadline for submissions to the Culture Foundation competition." I sat down at the computer. I sent the finished book
to Poland, and *The Mismatch* won the Culture Foundation
Prize.

When I found myself in Israel, I quickly put on the mask
that is worn here. I learned Hebrew in three months, in order
to become acclimatized, to be an Israeli. I knew that I was
starting out in a new direction and that I should forget what
had gone before. But that is not possible. The older you get,
the more you remember. You also have to keep making choic-
es constantly. You don't know whether to stay where you are,
or to keep moving. Are you in your homeland, or not? Until
in the end you conclude that the only place for neurotic Jews
is in Israel. So you stay here and talk to yourself. There is no
demand for neurotic Jews.

Do I cook cabbage soup at home in Jerusalem? That is how
one of my fictional characters found refuge. I cook. Cabbage
soup is an escape into Polishness. But it's all ambivalent. Israel
has a beautiful colour to it. I live in Jerusalem, the most beautiful place on earth. There are days, weeks, months, when I
feel like an Israeli all the time. When my daughter went into

the army and became an officer, I was so proud of her! But there are also other situations. In Poland, you know, people said, "You Jew!" Here I sometimes hear them say, "You Pole!"

My generation was born after the war. Some people say that we have no right to write about things we did not live through. That's true – it's the people who lived through the Holocaust that have the most right to it. But the problem of destruction also affects their children. I am thinking of a certain nightmarish sort of childhood, and of growing up in an atmosphere where there were taboo subjects. Let me tell you about a man who survived a concentration camp. Here, in Israel, he had a son who committed suicide in the army. The father also hanged himself. He could not live without his son. He supposedly hanged himself on a tree at Yad Vashem. He left behind a note saying, "We people from the Holocaust should not be allowed to have children."

When I eat soup, of course, I put the spoon in my mouth, not in my eye. Yet I have certain images within myself. I remember an uncle from Poland – I was a little girl when he came to see us in Wrocław. This uncle survived because he was a strongman. He could pull a nail out of a board with his teeth. When I asked him about the war, he cried like a baby.

These are traumatic experiences. I remember how the Yom Kippur war started. I was pregnant, and alone at home because my husband had gone into the army. My first impulse was to run to the mirror and put on makeup. Why? I had a vision of myself under the rubble. I looked like all those corpses I had seen in war films and documentaries. And I wanted to look nicer.

So these are things we can talk about, because they affect us. That is why there is an organization in Israel for the children of such parents.

Jewishness is a stigma. I look on it positively when I think of Tuwim or Słonimski, and negatively when I hear anti-Semitic opinions. Then the stigma drives me onto the barricades, to defend Jewishness. There are times when I would like to forget about that. To live somewhere in Australia, grow roses and not answer those damned questions.'

28 For Twelve Lilac Bushes

I have known the poetry of Łucja Pinczewska-Gliksman for several years. I knew that she was born near Kalisz. I asked my Israeli friends about her, and Irit Amiel told me her life-story, Miriam Akavia about her poetry, while Ryszard Löw sent me a copy of her work. Then I went to Opatówek. I asked Piotr Łuszczykiewicz of Kalisz to accompany me as I wandered there in search of something. I knew that his grandmother, Erna Wiewiórkowska, had worked in the Pinczewski doll factory. She was a bookkeeper, and in one of her poems Łucja Gliksman writes, 'Erna put everything down in the books.'

In Opatówek I met Marysia Posiłek. Her father Michał was a foreman in the Pinczewski factory. Among some old papers, she had come across a photograph of Anna Pinczewska, Łucja Gliksman's grandmother. The story of the Jewish inhabitants of Opatówek moved me so much that I wrote an article about it, and Marek Nowakowski of Poznań television shot a documentary film based on that article. We went to the local museum, where we found only one doll. Those dolls did not survive the turmoil of the war, or perhaps they simply went out of fashion. 'They were too fragile for those times,' Piotr said. 'They had china heads.'

The Pinczewskis came to Opatówek at the end of the nineteenth century. They bought some real estate on Długa Street and built a factory making dolls and wooden toys. Their toys won a medal at the 1898 St Petersburg Fair and a certificate at the 1900 Vienna Industrial Exhibition that entitled them to use the cross of honour and a gold medal. The factory was owned by the Pinczewski brothers, Maks and Natek. Łucja

Pinczewska-Gliksman is Maks' daughter. She studied Polish at Warsaw University and escaped to Lwów with her family when the war broke out. It was there that she received news of the tragic deaths of her brother Waldek and his wife, Irka Jezierska. They died in Belgium when they were run over by a drunken driver. Her youngest brother, Adam, was arrested after the arrival of the Soviet army. Łucja was deported in June 1940 to Kopieysk, beyond the Urals, where she, her mother and her brother Julek spent many months working in a coal-mine. After being released under the terms of the agreement between Stalin and the Polish government-in-exile, they travelled to Tadzhikistan, where Łucja found employment with the delegation of the government-in-exile. She set up a Polish school and an orphanage, and drew up a register of Polish families living in the Soviet Far East. In 1942 she reached Teheran with General Anders' army. That was where she was notified about the death of her youngest brother. She went on to the Middle East and, in spite of illness, worked as a culture and education official for the government-in-exile. She made her literary debut in a magazine called *The Pole in Iran*. After the war, she and her husband Jerzy Gliksman emigrated to the United States. She worked on a book about the Soviet camps, held classes with Slavic language students at the University of Chicago, and lectured on Soviet literature at Roosevelt University. She joined the staff of the Russian Institute at Harvard. After the death of her husband she came to Israel, where her ailing mother was living, as well as her sole surviving brother.

Having steeped myself in Opatówek, I packed my knapsack and flew to Tel Aviv. I had pictures of the Pinczewski home and factory with me, as well as my newspaper articles and a portrait of her grandmother.

I showed everything to Miriam Akavia. She phoned Łucja Gliksman and read her the story of the dolls from Opatówek. When Miriam put down the receiver, she said, 'Łucja wept.' We had an appointment for the following day, and I knew that I was on my way to meet an exceptional woman. Miriam is a good driver and it only took her a moment to find a parking space near Chen Street. We were in the very centre of the city, among houses built of concrete. They were put up in such a way that narrow strips of green separated one house from another. Łucja Gliksman lived on the second floor in one of those houses on Chen Street: a house just like all the others around, with small windows shielded by Venetian blinds, resembling in some way a prison or barracks building. I rang the doorbell. Łucja opened the door: a lady with white hair. She hugged me, as if we had known each other for years.

We sat down in the small living room, at a table with a white rose on it. I could see Leo Lipski through a door that was left ajar. He was bedridden, 'walled up in his own body'. His lively, sensitive eyes formed a contrast to his immobilized body. On the wall hung a stick from the times when he could still use it to move around. Now, he only read books. Or rather, he 'consumed them', as Tomasz Jastrun wrote. (It seemed to Jastrun that Leo Lipski ate the pages of the books.)

Łucja Gliksman met Lipski on a ship bound for Haifa in 1943. That word 'met' implies too much. She merely observed the man, a stranger and an outstanding writer, from the corner of her eye, without ever suspecting that fate would bring them together years later. When she settled in Israel, she became personally acquainted with Lipski. After the death of her mother and brother, she began taking care of the writer, whose health was steadily declining. In 1973 Łucja and Lipski travelled to Paris, where they met Giedroyc, Czapski and Herling-Grudziński. That was one of the last times he contended against the increasing immovability of his body. In the memoirs that he wrote years later in Contours, Lipski notes:

I am in Western Europe for the first time, chronically ill, having just undergone hip surgery, with all the pins visible on the X-rays. I am enraged at Paris, at a Europe that does not accept me ... I tell Łucja that I want to return home, that she can stay, but I want to go back to the besieged city. If I now recall Paris fondly, it is thanks to the people. Łucja phones the next morning: Jerzy Giedroyc, Czapski and many others are there ...We are waiting for Józef Czapski to visit after dinner. I too have recently begun referring to him by the familiar name

'Józio'. I have never laid eyes on him. He wrote to me after the publication of *Piotruś* ... When Łucja finally takes the elevator down to let Józio in, I go to the elevator and weep. I cover his face and hands with kisses.

In one of her letters, Łucja Gliksman told me about Poznań as she remembered it almost 60 years earlier. About the woods, the stream, the ravines. About the garden that led down to the pond and was full of fruit trees, lilac bushes, jasmine, clumps of strawberries and flowers. About the mullein growing on the far side of the railway track. The letter ended with the words, 'One can go on forever about what one loves.' As if she did not want to part from the place she loved or break off the conversation, she attached a poem entitled 'The Peatbog':

Sweet flag, bulrush, and mint grew by the pond,
Forget-me-not blossomed, shining with blue enamel,
But the turf absorbed everything and crept nearer,
Together with the chewed-up greenery, it lapped like a
    wave over the pond.

And my own life is thus absorbed by the past –
People, events, thoughts, feelings – in a word, every-
    thing,
And so the pond disappeared without a trace, the
    garden, the house, the memories,
Became a black, slimy, frustrated peatbog.

We are sitting around a table. It is swelteringly hot. I wonder if Łucja heard the echoes of the gunshots aimed at Icchak Rabin 'that day'. (It was only a few steps from their house.) Then, a moment later, I remember that I am in Tel Aviv. Łucja Pinczewska is leading me to the garden in Opatówek. We touch the blossoming trees and stroll between the flower patches. 'How many flowers there are!' I exclaim. And she reads me a poem about the campion among the grass, about the green meadows on the water. I ask what campion look like. 'Like carnations linked together,' replies Łucja. They had separated petals, in a colour that tended to lilac. They grew in the meadow because the forget-me-nots 'crowded them away' from the pond.

I ask her about Poland and her youth. 'I was in various places in Poland,' Łucja replies. 'In such lovely places as Zakopane and Cracow. But now Poland has shrunk to two localities: my native village and Warsaw. Those places are full of nostalgia. Especially Opatówek. When I was living in Washington, a representative of the B'nai B'rith called on my husband. He asked me, "What would you ask for if the Germans paid reparations?" I answered: "For enough money to buy twelve lilac bushes."

Almost 200 Jews lived in Opatówek before the war. Some were rich and some were poor. There was a rich man called Matusiak. Colette met his beautiful daughter in Belgium after the war. There was also a poor man called Matusiak, whose daughter had a child by a goy. The goyish father supposedly saved that child when the war came. On the square was a shop belonging to the Jew Tangowski. He sold percale and shoes. On Sunday, the peasants carried their shoes in their hands and only put them on in front of the church. Across from Tangowski's was Jarecki's shop. One of his daughters survived and went to live in Tel Aviv. I remember the Ejzner brothers. The older one was a Zionist and emigrated to Palestine. He corresponded with my brother. The younger one, Kuba, was our chauffeur. The Fajgin family lived in Opatówek. They had a grocery store: spices, coffee and sugar … There was Adler's shop – he was our lathe operator. His wife ran the shop, while their daughter helped Erna Wiewiórkowska at the factory. One of Adler's sons was a lawyer. The other was a livestock dealer in Poznań. Both of them survived. One of them visited me in Tel Aviv. It was Rywka Adler who told me that I was Jewish. "What about Anielcia, the daughter of our superintendent?" I asked her. "No, Anielcia's not," Rywka answered. "Poor Anielcia," I said.

The Fajgins had a daughter called Frania. She married a man who wanted to go to Palestine. He wanted to go, so he went. Frania died of a brain tumour in Israel. I went to see her before she died. We talked in Polish. Frania asked me, "Does Erna write?" I lied to her and said, "She writes, and she asked me to remember her to you." Then Frania asked, "Do you love Opatówek?" "Yes," I said, "I love it." "I love it too," she said. At that moment, she lost consciousness. Those were her last words.

They said that there was a village full of Jewish horse thieves nearby. Szmul Czarnożył supposedly married a woman from that village. He was a tinsmith. He was so poor that, out of pity, he was given a job as a night watchman in our factory and an apartment in the factory courtyard. He had two daughters, Lucia and Brońcia. When his wife was pregnant, my grandmother sent her additional food. But it turned out that she put a special pillow under her dress in order to get that extra food by fraud. My grandmother called Czarnożył in and asked him, "What do you need another child for?" And he answered, "Pardon me, but I have nothing to do with that." One thing worth knowing about Czarnożył is that he had the first volume of an encyclopedia and learned all the words beginning with "a" by heart.'

When Polish children in Opatówek wanted to make fun of Jewish children, they chanted, 'The Jewess sells eggs/See how she begs/She sells thread and twine/See her bare behind.' More than 60 years on, Łucja Gliksmann remembers that rhyme. She is an educated lady who once frequented the 'Gentry' café and was a professor at American universities. What is more, the rhyme only came back to her when she settled in Israel, when she thought she had forgotten about the Jewish butcher Szlamiak, and about the percale that Tangowski sold. That was when she wrote a bitter, pessimistic poem about her brothers from Opatówek and Warsaw:

How ashamed am I now
That I was once a stranger
To you: dark, bearded Jews
And small boys in side-curls.
Pale Jewish women with baskets,
Faces over the books in the prayer house,
In the little stores, workshops, and stalls,
Sad Jewish streets.

Killed in Treblinka, Majdanek,
Ascended as smoke into heaven,
Never knowing a funeral
Living only in memory
So many years away,
Come back to me all of you,
O Jewish brothers, for today it hurts
That too late you are dear to me.

Łucja went on: 'My great-grandfather, Izrael Fryde, owned the village of Brzeziny. A German bought it from him, and he took the money and bought a building in Kalisz. Izrael's children were Joel, Daniel, Zelig, Jakub and Anna, my grandmother, who took her husband's surname, Pinczewski.

I recall my grandfather's sister, Anna Berman. She had two daughters, Regina and Róża. They married Germans. Regina probably died. Róża managed get her husband out of the Dachau camp, and they emigrated to London. My grandfather, Abraham Pinczewski, also had brothers. One of them, Menachem, was very religious and sent his only son to the *yeshiva*. My grandfather's other brother lived in Ostrava in Moravia. Then there was a third brother, Joel, who had exceptionally gifted children. Marysia became a botanist and Witek and Kuba were both neurologists. They all died.

When the First World War broke out, the Germans arrested 24 citizens, including two Jews: Frenkl and my grandfather. They shot them on 4 August 1914, and refused to allow them to be buried. But my aunt stole my grandfather's body during the night and a quiet funeral was held.

The name Fryde appears several times in Aleksander Pakentreger's book on the Jews of Kalisz. Pakentreger writes about Adolf (Abel) Fryde, a sponsor of the Talmud Torah. Adolf Fryde was from Kalisz, but moved to Capetown in South Africa, where he amassed a great fortune. When he visited Kalisz in 1922, the board made a presentation to him about the sorry state of the school. Fryde then gave an undertaking to guarantee that the poorest pupils would have full board and lodging, including meals with meat. Pakentreger also mentions a merchant named Zelig Fryde, vice-president of the Jewish community in the 1920s. In the October 1924 elections to the leadership of the Jewish community, Zelig Fryde of Aguda was elected chairman. He was 65 years old, and remained in office for five years, until his death in 1929. The Aguda party in Kalisz was founded in March 1920. Its slogan was "*Hevei mispalel bishlomo shel malchus*" (Pray for the welfare of the state).'

The girls in the boarding house wrote in their albums, "Laugh before people, and weep only in private. Be light on your feet, but never in your conduct." And I laugh before people, but I weep in private. I can feel death standing beside me. I lost all those I loved. When my husband was dying, I still had illusions. I did not believe in his death. I watched over him and never went out. Only once did I go downstairs to the store. One time. I remember standing in the hallway and knowing that he was waiting for me. I thought, is anyone as unfortunate as I am? And yet I would want it to always be that way. If only I could still worry about him that way. I could go on suffering, if only he were alive. However, it was not to be. Of all those I loved, only stones remain:

> And what was it for
> What good did it do me
> – Life?
> All that remain
> Are these grey stones
> Beneath which you sleep
> And what was it for
> Why was I clothed
> – In existence??
> All that I need
> All that I wait for
> Are these grey stones.

When I was registering Poles in Tadzhikistan, a Jew in a long beard came up to me. He sat down beside me and began to talk affectionately of Poland. I was surprised, and interrupted his monologue to say, "I have a right to feel nostalgic, because I was raised speaking Polish and graduated from a Polish university. But you are from a little Jewish *shtetl*. You had little contact with Poles. And you must have encountered anti-Semitism. So why do you speak so well of Poland?" And he answered: "Our brother Poles were often bad, but our mother Poland was always good."'

29 The Poznańers of Tel Aviv

It is a sweltering evening. Krystyna and Henio Kronenberg and I are standing at Jurek Janowski's door. We knock, and a moment later we are saying hello to Noach Lasman, Adek Redlich and Olek Abramowicz. Jurek sets us Poznańers around a long table in his garden. There is Polish vodka and Israeli beer. That's good, I think. As always, I am afraid of shedding a tear, and emotion stifles my voice. I know that these Poznańers are a tough bunch: they've been around. Today, they're all over 70 and they know what life is about. They can all remember Dobski's café, Hirschlik's restaurant – and their flight from Poznań in 1939.

Olek remembers how they used to beg for lead letters at the nearby printer's – perfect for shooting from a slingshot. Heniek asks, 'Do you remember Karol Szorstki? He lived across from Moszkowicz's elegant restaurant. Karol made a bow and arrow and he shot out one of Moszkowicz's windows. His father paid for the glass.'

Jurek remembers the smell of iris toffee. He must have really liked it, because he wouldn't share it with Noach Lasman when he was boy. All those years ago, and Lasman, who now lives in America, won't let him forget. So Jurek bought a big pack of toffees when he was in Poland, and now they're waiting for Lasman in Israel. He imagines how he'll put the toffees out on the table when Lasman visits him in Tel Aviv and say, 'Here, help yourself.' And then everything will be like it was back when they used to meet up on the corner of Żydowska Street on the way to Mrs Propst's school.

In general, Jurek is a big joker. 'Or was,' his wife adds, back when he lived in Poznań. 'I once went to the Wedel shop on

Freedom Square,' he recalls. 'I said to the shop girl, "Give me 200 grams of those chocolates, 100 grams of those in red wrappers, and 150 more grams of those bronze-coloured ones." When she had finished weighing it all out, I said, "Excuse me, Miss, but I've been thinking about it, and I don't feel like anything sweet." And I ran out of the shop.'

Adek says, 'And I made a kind of spring that I would put in the crack between the floor and the bottom of the door. I would get up at five in the morning, fit the spring under the neighbour's door, ring the doorbell and run. The lady of the house would usually wake up and come out into the hallway. In the morning, believe me, she did not look as if she'd just stepped out of the Dior catalogue. Once she came out into the hallway, the spring would make the door close on its own. Sometimes there was no one inside to let her back in, because she was at home alone.'

Olek had a Dobermann pinscher. On his way back from school, he would stand outside their apartment on Marcinkowski Street and whistle to his mother. She would open the door and the dog would come running downstairs. Olek would then safely go through the entranceway, where it was easiest to get beaten up, and up the stairs. He was afraid of the boys in the courtyard, who were not particularly fond of little Jews. He also recalls how they wrote something in *The Spokesman* about 'stinking Jews', and somebody broke the windows in his father's store.

Jurek gets emotional when talking about his Paderewski school. He admits that there were only four Jews there – him, his brother and two other boys. In 1939, for some reason that he cannot recall, a 'pogrom' was organized at the school. His two friends were beaten up, and even threatened with lynching. But nobody laid a hand on the Janowski brothers. 'Maybe it was because we were well-liked,' Jurek hypothesizes. In the aftermath of that incident, their class teacher, a tall, handsome man named Woźniak who was a Polish patriot, told his charges, 'I can understand it if somebody doesn't like Jews, but a true Pole does not act that way.'

197

They were not religious. Of course, they went to the synagogue on Yom Kippur and each of them had his bar mitzvah and gladly accepted presents on the occasion, but they were not very interested in the religion of their forefathers. They belonged to the Zionist Hashomer Hatzair organization and dreamed of going to Palestine. When Olek Abramowicz went on vacation to Krynica with his mother, he stopped off at the station in Cracow. There, for the first time in his life, he saw a large group of little children dressed in black. He ran to his mother to tell her about these strange people wearing 'pots' on their heads. When he arrived in Jerusalem years later, he saw that there were many people there wearing 'pots'.

Adek had a different kind of adventure after arriving in Israel. He saw a strangely dressed Jew on a bus. Some sort of 'fringe' stuck out from under his coat. Adek thought it was underwear. He was just about to draw this to the man's attention, but his wife rescued him from embarrassment at the last moment and explained to him the complicated garments of the observant Jew.

Jurek remembers a story about a Jew who travelled from Cracow to Poznań on business. When the Hasid got off the train, he noticed how everyone was staring at him with goggling eyes. 'What are you all gaping at?' he asked. 'Haven't you ever seen anybody from Cracow before?'

They talk about their children, who are scattered all over the world. Sometimes they fly to Poland with them. Adek does so. They rent a car and drive to Cracow, Białystok, Warsaw, Treblinka, Chełmno and Birkenau. Poznań is the final stop on this journey back to their youth, as Olek says, 'the icing on the cake'. When they get there, they walk along the streets of their childhood, knocking on apartment doors and explaining to the surprised tenants that they lived there 60 years ago with their parents, brothers and sisters. Sometimes, they write letters to the president of Poland. They tell him how much it hurts to be forgotten. About the plaques torn off the synagogues, about the Jewish schools, almost all of whose pupils died and who are now forgotten in their beloved Poznań.

Someone hums a song that was sung on the streets before

the war: 'At the birth of little Moses, *oy-oy-oy*/Poznań hardly smelled of roses, *oy-oy-oy*.' Henio asks: 'And what was it we sang in Mrs Propst's Jewish school?' Jurek picks up the melody and then the words of the Catholic hymn, 'At the First Light of Dawn'. When Jurek has finished, we sing 'God Who Poland …' and 'The White Roses in Blossom'. It is almost midnight now and the reminiscing has made everyone nostalgic. I think to myself: 'All I have to do now is get these Poznańers to pose for a group photo.'

Saying goodbye is a long, complicated process. Finally, 'the big guy', Olek Abramowicz, comes over to me. 'You know,' he says, 'when I left Poznań, the streets were so wide and the houses so high. When I went back 50 years later, those same streets were narrower and those houses lower. Only the Warta River flowed as lazily as ever. Can you tell me where it all went? Isn't anyone ever going to sing the Kol Nidre again in the synagogue on Stawna Street, and look at the flickering light of the candles on the wall? Where is that Poznań that we've dragged with us all the way to Tel Aviv and Jerusalem? Can you tell me?'